Not Fit T

Steve Davis

Not Fit To Govern

Essays on Liberal Democracy

Acknowledgements

Earlier versions of these essays were published in the following issues of *Voice*:
'A Brief Encounter With Liberty' – *Voice* 19
'Power to the People' – *Voice* 20
'Too Good To Be True' – *Voice* 16
'Creation Myths' – *Voice* 23
'Shall We Eat the Cabin Boy? An Examination of Liberal Ethics' – *Voice* 15
'Francis Fukuyama and the Myths of Liberal Democracy' – *Voice* 3
'Defending Society from Attacks by the State' – *Voice* 13
'It's All About Property, Right?' – *Voice* 18
'Free Traders Old And New' – *Voice* 8
'Dark Lords' – *Voice* 17
'Puppies And Other Important People' – *Voice* 14
'Liberty, Equality, Fraternity' – *Voice* 9
'The Collective Illusion' – *Voice* 5
'Rethinking the Counterculture' – *Voice* 21

Not Fit To Govern: Essays on Liberal Democracy
ISBN 978 1 74027 541 5
Copyright © Steve Davis 2009

First published 2009
Reprinted 2017

GINNINDERRA PRESS
PO Box 3461 Port Adelaide SA 5015
www.ginninderrapress.com.au

Contents

Introduction

The essays in this volume originally appeared over a period of some years in *Voice* magazine, published by Ginninderra Press in Canberra. All were published well before the global financial turmoil of October 2008, to which all are linked. Other essays in *Voice* covered a variety of topics, but those appearing here developed a common theme, a belief that representative democracy has not just outlived its usefulness, but has become a danger to the survival of humanity itself.

The reasons for this are many, but most would belong in the three following categories. First, the capacity of the system to be manipulated by vested interests; second, its innate intolerance of and aggressiveness towards alternative social models; and third, the inability of the system to deal with national and global crises of its own creation.

The manipulation of the system by vested interests, as occurred in the lead-up to the financial turmoil of October 2008 has been a feature of modern democracy from day one, this feature having its origins deep in British history, well before the modern concept of democracy emerged.

The innate aggressiveness and intolerance of the system also has its origins in British history, due to the formation among an intellectual class in Britain of an ideology of individualism which has free market economics as its principal modern expression. So successful has the promotion of individualism been that modern democracy is now referred to as liberal democracy, liberalism being political code for economic individualism.

The inability of the system to deal with crises of its own creation is well illustrated for Australian readers by the Murray-Darling water catchment fiasco, which grew out of control due to lobbying by parliamentary representatives, on behalf of constituents, for water allocations beyond a sustainable level.

It might surprise some readers that parliamentary democracy has been the cause of these problems. I hope this collection will show that modern democracy, far from being a foundation of stability, is actually the source of much of the instability that currently plagues the globe.

A Brief Encounter with Liberty

One of the advantages of entering advanced middle age lies in acquiring the ability to detect social trends not apparent to younger observers. Technological advances are so rapid that anyone past primary school age can be aware of developments, but trends in the way society thinks require observation over a considerable period.

Those readers who can remember the 1950s and 60s, the height of the Cold War, will recall that during that era the Western propaganda machine rarely missed an opportunity to use almost any aspect of Soviet life as evidence not only of economic inefficiency, but of moral deficiency and brutality. It was as though our cultural managers took the view that we needed constant reminders of the superiority of Western culture, blissfully ignorant of the fact that the truly superior need no such assurance. One of the now rather amusing examples of this misuse of the news media was the shock and horror that was expressed in reports that Soviet women worked full-time and placed their children in child-care facilities during working hours. Some of these child-care facilities were even situated in the workplace so that mothers could have contact with their children during work breaks, a barbarous practice that would not be tolerated in any civilised society. As we now watch our politicians fall over themselves to appear to be doing all they can to provide child-care services for full-time working mums, we can only conclude that the Soviets were ahead of their time!

But this example of the West emulating Soviet practices once considered backward and unacceptable has a serious aspect. The steady move by governments in general to assume centralised control of all aspects of social life, coupled with the steady erosion of freedoms, will lead, if unchecked, to a totalitarian world, for the example is far from isolated.

We formerly condemned the Soviets for the practice of sending dissidents and political prisoners to isolated detention camps, yet our closest ally, with the support of the Howard government, attempted to hold prisoners, including an Australian, on an inaccessible island without trial and without recourse to the justice system. Our very own gulag.

We formerly condemned the Soviets for their repression of independent labour unions, yet the Howard government neutralised a significant vehicle for popular dissent by legislating to render unions here as ineffective as their Soviet counterparts.

We formerly condemned the Soviets for their indoctrination of the populace to a particular world-view, yet the Howard government had plans in place for the compulsory indoctrination of Australian schoolchildren to a 'factual' Australian history based on the virtues of Christianity. (Here are a few of the volumes of facts that won't get a run in Howard's history: the Gallipoli hero Simpson was a radical left-wing unionist; most liberals at the time of Federation believed in a fair distribution of wealth; unionised workplaces are generally healthier and wealthier than non-unionised; Robert Menzies was a fawning anglophile who put British interests ahead of the interests of Australians; the first returned servicemen's organisations in Australia were labour unions; the Communist Party of Australia, portrayed at the time as being extremist irresponsible and immoral, was at the forefront of many social issues now considered mainstream and highly moral; and we hid the shame of our discriminatory immigration policy by using English language exams set at university level to unfairly exclude applicants from non-preferred countries.)

We formerly condemned the Soviets for their control of the news media, but today in the world's most powerful democracy, events that do not conform to the view of the ruling elite are withheld from the people, a trend now increasingly noticeable in the Australian media. The US Congress is at this moment considering a bill that would prevent internet services at universities and colleges from providing access to sites other than those approved by government. If enacted, this would follow the Chinese government's lead in outright control of internet services.

We formerly condemned the Soviets for maintaining a one-party state, yet it's now widely accepted, with some amusement, that the US is also a one-party state, the Republicans and Democrats being two wings of a party of business. What's not so amusing is that at the time of George W. Bush's first presidential campaign, not only were presidential candidates from parties other than Republican and Democrat prevented from taking part in the televised debates, they were excluded from the room, a brazen exercise in thought control.

But totalitarian trends come from the right as well as the left of politics. The noted US historian William Ebenstein, who studied and wrote extensively on the history of totalitarian states, found the following to be typical features of the fascist outlook: irrationalism or the distrust of both reason and sceptical reflection, the affirmation of inequality as an ideal, a readiness to lie and to resort to violence, the principle of leadership ('in a conflict between the leader and the people the will of the leader prevails...'), the enforcement of orthodoxy and conformity, the elimination of collective bargaining in the workplace, a high value placed on discipline and obedience, and opposition to international organisation and world peace. It's not difficult to find all of these features in the recent actions of our government and of our allies, and Ebenstein could have added the demonising and mistreatment of selected minorities, also a feature of our recent past.

Of course it's openly conceded that limits on freedom have flowed from the alleged need to protect Western society from the threat of terrorism, but we should not accept such nonsense for a moment. As others have pointed out, the best way to reduce global terrorism is to stop participating in it, but it's clear from our activities in Iraq that such an option is not even considered. It was Joseph Goebbels who, as a prisoner of the Allies, informed his interrogators that the success of Nazi propaganda was due to the creating of official enemies to induce a powerful element of fear in the population, at which point people accept any measures alleged to offer protection against those enemies. Our latest foreign adventure is just one more instance of a script that has been faithfully followed ever since, and at the time of writing yet another tiny impoverished Asian nation is being depicted as a threat to the great powers. (Their missiles could even reach Australia, don't yer know!)

This drift towards totalitarianism should not come as a surprise. The dominant political outlook in the world today, liberalism, has a history and philosophical underpinning that compels a move in this direction. Of equal significance, our history for much of the last thousand years or more has been one of enforced conformity to the narrow demands of both monarch and Church. Only the twentieth century saw the emergence of something approaching genuine liberty, some considerable period after the Enlightenment saw liberty appear, in theory only, as a serious social force. As we begin the twenty-first century, our short-lived liberties are being sacrificed on two fronts, to appease market forces, and to the need to protect us from enemies our guardians have not only created, but which they desperately need to preserve.

If there's one lesson to be learnt from the struggle for freedom, it's that the struggle never ends, and as long as liars and warmongers have the respect of the masses, as long as the people get their knowledge of the world from corporate media outlets, as long as children are indoctrinated by the state then we are living in some strange, dream-like twilight world, we cannot call ourselves free, we can barely call ourselves human. To live lives of passivity and compliance, to allow others to decide questions of right and wrong because we're told it's a nasty world out there is not to be human, it's to live at the animal level. Have we come all this way, have those before us shed blood sweat and tears in the name of independence and liberty so that we can merely exist, unthinking, like bees or ants in a colony? So that half a world away people we have never met, who wish us no harm, are killed and maimed and reduced to utter despair on our behalf, so that we can grow sleek and fat while enjoying the illusion of security?

The human story is of hard-won progress that was earned by living for ideals that go far beyond the satisfaction of bodily needs, yet that is exactly what our managers are telling us our focus should be. We are told to be relaxed and comfortable so that others can get on with the job of managing the world without interference. So that they can saddle us with inefficient nuclear power generation subsidised by silent, submissive taxpayers, so they can turn children into sub-humans by locking them in detention centres to be molested and abused, so they can wage wars of conquest for control of resources essential to an industrial era that is so far past its use-by date that it now poses a threat to human survival. It's time we started planning for the next stage in human progress, for the end of managerial democracy and the beginning of a golden age when people the world over become truly free, when we have the courage to live for ideals, the courage to be human.

Power to the People

It should be painfully obvious to any thinking person that parliamentary or representative democracy has lost all legitimacy as a useful social structure. When elected governments can wage war against the wishes of the electors, and can surrender power and authority to unelected anti-social corporate ideologues, then clearly the time has come to move on. This raises the question as to the form that should be taken by the next structure, but before that question is answered the reasons for the failure of representative democracy must be found to ensure that they do not live on with the evolutionary process.

The thwarting of democratic aspirations has been remarkably successful; a complex, expensive, long-term project in the manipulation of people's thinking to achieve what our managers termed the 'manufacturing of consent', or the convincing of people that the interests of the dominant class are actually the interests of the masses. This was the challenge that democratic ideals presented to those in power; unable to derail the democratic groundswell they learned to live with it, learned to manage democracy for their own narrow ends.

A variety of techniques and concepts have been used to carry out the project, ranging from the purely technical such as mass communication, even naked force, through to the psychological such as fear, prejudice and the conversion of elected representatives to the ranks of the elite. We've heard a lot in the past about the containment of communism, but that was merely the tip of the iceberg. The really big exercise, the ongoing campaign that involves a huge investment in time and resources, is the containment of democracy.

We should be alarmed by the fact that in the US the democratically elected president of Venezuela, Hugo Chavez, who has made no attempt to reconstruct or socialise the private sector in general or the independent news media in particular, is referred to as a communist, from which we can infer that for US elites and opinion-makers, democracy and communism are interchangeable terms. Why should this alarm us? It demonstrates the contempt held by elite opinion for what most people perceive democracy to be and contempt for an administration that actually works to improve the lot of its people. It's evidence of the lengths that are taken, the dishonesty that's involved and the paranoia that drives the control of public opinion. This program has been so effective that it has grown to become an industry in itself, pervading all aspects of social life, and yet it is, for many people, a reality of which they are completely unaware.

But if the powerful have themselves recognised that manipulation of public opinion is the crucial factor in the exercise of power, that they need the consent of the masses, then clearly the ultimate source of power is not money or guns or force, but the people themselves. It's the people who give power to the rulers. All that we need to do therefore is to come up with a democratic structure which is impervious to the influence of contrary interests. This raises an interesting little historical footnote. Anselme Bellegarrigue was an early anarchist who arrived back in France from the US on the morning of the revolution of 1848. He was not impressed. According to his account, a young national guardsman boasted to him that this time the workers would not be robbed of their victory. 'They have robbed you already of your victory,' replied Bellegarrigue. 'Have you not named a government?' This comes almost as a shock, so narrow is our view of democracy, so the value of the story lies in its confirmation that a serious weakness in democratic concepts was detectable from the very beginning. We have to change the way we think about democracy if it is to serve our needs, and this change becomes more urgent with each passing year as representative democracy increasingly becomes a destructive force in world affairs.

What we have been manipulated into accepting, and into believing that it's the only option, is the lazy person's democracy. An irresponsible democracy in which we don't have to think too much or too hard. A once every three or four years democracy in which our managers allow us to vote for those representatives who will continue to pursue policies and projects that exploit and endanger and harm us.

So is there an alternative? Anselme Bellegarrigue with his fondness for the paradoxical quote might provide us with a clue. With some flair he declared that 'Anarchy is order.' What could this mean?

For a start, anarchy does not refer to an absence of government, but rather to the absence of a ruler. The order he referred to in the absence of a ruler is the order that comes into being naturally, spontaneously, when people follow their social instincts and form associations based on mutual need, mutual aid and mutual respect. An order that is ecological in its operations, an order that evolves, that changes with circumstances, but which retains at all times the essential feature of stability. An order based on moral conduct. Such a social structure would by its very nature be decentralised, regional and local in its operations, and therefore far more likely to be immune to those outside interests that might try to commandeer it. In short, a structure owned and operated by its constituents.

'But we need a strong government and powerful friends to protect us.' some will cry. Well, actually, we don't. The Swiss have got by quite nicely by adopting a neutral position that has been satisfactorily respected to date, and the Kiwi withdrawal from the ANZUS treaty did not, despite predictions, result in the end of civilisation as we know it. Furthermore, a society based on cooperation is likely to have a far lower crime rate than a society driven by greed, conflict and aggression. This all seems very theoretical, even wildly fanciful, driven by wishful thinking and invalid assumptions regarding the essential goodness of human nature, but it may well be that future circumstances could bring such an arrangement into being by a completely unplanned process of evolution.

Take the time, for just a moment, to imagine a world in which the economy is not driven by power generated from fossil fuels. A world in which power is obtained from renewable resources would be an empowering world, for individuals and communities would not be dependent on, and at the mercy of, centralised systems of electricity generation; they would generate their own. They would be independent of global and national economies for a major contributor to living standards. This would immediately rob powerbrokers (in all meanings of the word) of their influence over the masses. It would lead to a more stable, friendly, cooperative world, for it would eliminate a major source of conflict and erode the shackles of economic domination.

I believe that this is recognised by our managers and is the reason for the sudden interest in nuclear power that has been put on the agenda the world over. They do not want nuclear power to take over when global warming can no longer be ignored because nuclear is clean and green as they falsely claim; they want it because it requires a centralised, and therefore disempowering, distribution system. They also know that a shift away from coal for electricity generation will hasten the shift away from fossil fuels in general. In short, the intended principal purpose of an expanded nuclear power industry is the entrenchment of the privileges of the dominant class.

A society that converted to power generation from renewable resources would undergo a psychological transformation; confidence would build, communities would become vibrant and vital instead of being hamstrung by the constricting web of state influence, and this would induce the next step in social evolution. Localised power generation owned and operated by communities would enable people to see the untapped potential that lies in community-based enterprise; this in turn would generate further industrial development owned and operated by communities. The influence of globalised interests would wane; trade agreements would be negotiated at the local level rather than national, and would be more sensitive to local needs in the areas of culture and environment. Gradually, the nation-state would be seen as increasingly irrelevant, a cumbersome parasite and a check on human growth and potential. At that point the vision of the early anarchists, the vision of a true democracy based on voluntary association and mutual respect, just might become a reality.

Of course such a fundamental change in social structure would not result from a single factor such as oil depletion, and even though the change might take years to consolidate, conditions conducive to development in a certain direction are needed well beforehand. Those conditions are influencing events right now. In early September 2006, PBS television (a US network not noted for biting the hand that feeds it) screened a news segment titled 'The Disposable Worker', which covered ten years of corporate downsizing in the USA. The program targeted the downsizing myths (their term, not mine) that corporate America had foisted on the public – for example that after a few years the economy would reach equilibrium and the downsizing cease, and that the stronger economy would provide equivalent jobs for those laid off – and exposed these as pure propaganda. It was clear that not only is there a growing disenchantment in the US with the workings of the capitalist system, but that sections of the news media are prepared to cover such issues. That's not to suggest that the US is ripe for revolution, but they do have a rich tradition of community solidarity from the colonial era, a tradition that could well inspire a movement in the direction indicated and may have already done so, the virtual bio-region concept being a case in point.

Too Good To Be True

There's an old saying in financial circles to the effect that if an investment proposition sounds too good to be true then it probably is. This is a piece of good common sense, born of countless high hopes and dashed expectations, the accumulated wisdom of generations of investors looking for an easy path to financial security. Of course there's no easy path to managing economic affairs at even the personal level, let alone the national level. It would seem reasonable to expect therefore that those managing the economic affairs of nations would be aware of just a little investment history and act accordingly with due prudence, but the opposite is the case. Elected governments, economic advisors, political commentators, global financial institutions, you name it: they are all playing along with the most obvious confidence trick in human history, a proposition that we should be walking away from because it's just too good to be true.

It goes like this. Because those pushing the cult of individualism know their outlook is socially destructive and therefore unacceptable to the public in its raw form, they've had to invent an ethical basis to justify their claims. The falsehood they came up with was this: when individuals are encouraged to pursue their own selfish impulses, any disadvantage suffered by unwitting or unwilling participants as this process rolls on can be excused as the net effect is beneficial to society as a whole. So not only does this process have an alleged ethical foundation, it's alleged to have the further uplifting benefit of encouraging the losers to put in the extra effort needed to become winners. And it makes governing so easy because all you have to do to serve society and, as is often implied, carry out God's will, is to put in place structures that encourage the greedy and the grasping.

Now you probably should not accept that this laughable nonsense is the keystone of modern economic philosophy and policy, or that sober and respectable elected representatives would embrace so transparent a fantasy, so to assuage your understandable doubts as to my honesty I offer the following quotes, some of which, significantly, have circulated unchanged for centuries.

Adam Smith on entrepreneurs:

> by directing…industry in such a manner as its produce may be of the greatest value, he intends only his own gain, and he is in this, as in many other cases, led by an invisible hand to promote an end which was no part of his intention. Nor is it always the worse for the society that it was no part of it. By pursuing his own interest he frequently promotes that of the society more effectually than when he really intends to promote it.

Social philosopher Jeremy Bentham reversed the issue somewhat, demonstrating his ignorance by stating that immoral action is 'a miscalculation of self-interest' (the unspoken flipside of which is that all well-calculated self-interest is morally justified) and continued,

> The community is a fictitious body composed of the individual persons who are considered as constituting as it were its members. The interest of the community then is, what? The sum of the interests of the members who composed it.

Even the poet Alexander Pope was carried away by the deception, being moved to wax lyrical:

> Thus God and Nature link'd the gen'ral frame, And bade Self-love and Social be the same.

But it was the late twentieth century that saw this type of thinking really flower, with characters such as Ayn Rand, who for a period exerted significant influence on an impressionable Malcolm Fraser among others, producing a prodigious output of propaganda devoted to the concept of greed as a virtue, with volumes of comments along these lines:

> Make no mistake about it…capitalism and altruism cannot coexist in the same man or in the same society.

If any civilization is to survive, it is the morality of altruism that men have to reject.

Thankfully Fraser did not get too carried away by sentiments such as these, but Howard's industrial reforms had Ayn Rand written all over them, with the government trying to reduce workplaces to bear-pits of competing individuals.

Rand's pseudo-intellectualism was given respectability by the Austrian school of economists comprised of such figures as Ludwig von Mises, who came up with pearls such as this:

Neither love nor charity nor any other sympathetic sentiments but rightly understood selfishness is what originally impelled man to adjust himself to the requirements of society.

This loose grouping had another feature in common: tenacity. For years they represented the extreme right of political thought, the libertarian lunatic fringe, but their fierce self-belief paid off. Think-tanks devoted to promoting their economic madness now dominate the debate in the US, to the extent that more mainstream figures, such as the hugely influential Milton Friedman, began using the same intemperate language with purely political intent, as in this howler from 1994:

The free market is the only mechanism that has ever been discovered for achieving participatory democracy.

Just as an aside, it should not be forgotten that this type of intemperate language, bordering on the sociopathic, used first by extreme figures such as Ayn Rand and Enoch Powell, is now the norm for many mainstream commentators here in Australia. Their extremism is evident in their intolerance to opposing argument and their belief that no other view but their own should be entitled to public expression. That concept from the Enlightenment of disputing what is said but defending its right to be heard is completely foreign to them. This journalism of intolerance and invective is not confined to Australia. Right-wing US commentator Anne Coulter, portrayed in *The Australian* as 'the pin-up girl for the hard right' once described delegates to a Democratic convention as 'the spawn of Satan', and recently attacked her ally G.W. Bush for his choice of replacement for a Supreme Court retiree, saying that Bush now has no right to say 'trust me' and that 'he was elected to represent the American people not to be a dictator for eight years', and all this because the nominated replacement was not a clone of Coulter herself. Her views on terrorism are informative:

Not all Muslims may be terrorists, but all terrorists are Muslims.

Being nice to people is, in fact, one of the incidental tenets of Christianity, as opposed to other religions whose tenets are more along the lines of 'kill everyone who doesn't smell bad and doesn't answer to the name Mohammed.'

Clearly we are dealing here with a fundamentalism that is dangerous and primitive, a belief that the democratic process is only legitimate when it serves an ever-narrowing sectional interest.

While Friedman at least tried to come up with some innovative justifications for old prejudices, the recycling of the ideas of classical economists is the standard fare of most free market activists today, for example this from *Capitalist Magazine*: 'The public good [properly defined] is promoted best by people pursuing their own private interests', paraphrasing Adam Smith as if dubious assumptions can be validated by repetition.

The unreasonable influence enjoyed by economic libertarians would be problematic enough, but here in Australia the situation is much worse. Rupert Murdoch has endorsed the extremism of these beliefs, as guest speaker in 1994 informing the rigidly right-wing Centre for Independent Studies that 'the principles of classical liberalism are fundamental to our civilisation' (or to put it in decoded language, 'class discrimination is fundamental to our schemes') and telling his biographer William Shawcross that libertarianism means 'as much individual responsibility as possible, as little government as possible, as few rules as possible'. The dissemination of these extreme views, formerly the province of the rabid right, is now a deliberate function of his media outlets. As a former editor of Murdoch's *Sunday Times* Andrew Neil wrote in 1983, 'Rupert expects his papers to stand broadly for what he believes.' *The Australian* newspaper has been perhaps the most active in this regard, pursuing an editorial policy favorable to economic rationalism for decades, and regularly publishing opinion articles produced by US think-tanks. Murdoch's domination of the media in this country, and his willingness to put pressure on governments, has resulted in profound changes in public opinion and perception.

Yet the situation is not without paradox. Friedrich von Hayek, darling of the libertarians, seems to refute the foundations of individualism with the following interpretation of the individual's relation to society:

> it is largely because civilization enables us constantly to profit from knowledge which we individually do not possess and because each individual's use of his particular knowledge may serve to assist others unknown to him in achieving their ends, that men as members of civilized society can pursue their individual ends so much more successfully than they could alone.

When the basics of individualism are expressed rationally as Hayek does here, it sounds more akin to collectivism. And in *The Fatal Conceit*, published in 1988, Hayek writes,

> To understand our civilization, one must appreciate that the extended order resulted not from human design or intention but spontaneously: it arose from unintentionally conforming to certain traditional and largely moral practices, many of which men tend to dislike, whose significance they usually fail to understand, whose validity they cannot prove, and which have nonetheless fairly rapidly spread by means of an evolutionary selection – the comparative increase of population and wealth – of those groups that happened to follow them. The unwitting, reluctant, even painful adoption of

these practices kept these groups together, increased their access to valuable information of all sorts, and enabled them to be 'fruitful, and multiply, and replenish the earth, and subdue it' (Genesis 1:28). This process is perhaps the least appreciated facet of human evolution.

If we can put aside the biblical allusions and a couple of arguable points for a moment, this is surely evolution from a socialist perspective.

But it was the noted Australian economist Barry Hughes who pointed out the weakness in the libertarian case when he reminded all who would listen that 'Only when the pursuit of self-interest remains the preserve of the few does the system remain workable.' We can see the truth of that verified in the venomous attacks on unions that pursue the self-interest of members. It's not that capitalism is an exclusive club, although that might play some part in the psychology. The plain fact, well understood, is that capitalism cannot handle wealth for the many at even the most modest level, as inflation spins out of control. The exclusiveness is an operational necessity, so long as we operate with tunnel vision and little imagination.

Perhaps it would be best to close with a word from John Maynard Keynes, who made a derisive comment to the effect that capitalism rests on the amazing assumption that the most wicked of men, performing the most wicked of acts, produce benefits for the whole of society. Like Keynes, we should not accept that proposition. It's too simple; it's an abrogation of responsibility, as a central plank of economic policy it's an admission that governing for the good of society is just too difficult. It's the mind-set of those who have a budget surplus at their fingertips and cannot think of anything more useful to do with it than appeal to the base instincts of the electorate by floating the prospect of a tax cut or increasing the size of the military. Can we really serve society best, and slip one foot inside heaven's door, by recklessly pursuing our own narrow wants? Not only is that just too good to be true, it symbolises the outlook of those who are not fit to govern.

Creation Myths

The term 'wealth creation' has always bothered me. It's tossed about with gay abandon by the ruling elite, it's included in the preamble to the Liberal Party federal platform, there's barely a day goes by when it's not heard on national television and they use it for good reason: it contains a number of subliminal but very powerful messages. The first is the claim that certain individuals actually create wealth, a myth that we'll look at in detail later. The second, which follows from the first, is that if a wealth-creating class exists then there must be a wealth-consuming class; in short, the rest of us make up a parasitical class. There's a multitude of conclusions that can be drawn from this: there's the obvious superiority of the wealth creators, there's the debt the rest of us owe the wealth creators, the need for acceptance of their wisdom and decision-making capabilities, their natural right to enjoyment of a greater share of the world's resources. We could go on forever in similar vein but, as all such conclusions follow from the claim that wealth can be created, it's time we put it to the test.

Karl Marx and the other great socialist thinkers of the nineteenth century put the matter succinctly with their conclusion that capital is no more than stored labour. If this is true, and I believe that generally it is, then it follows that large accumulations of capital are of doubtful legitimacy for they must be made up of the labour of many. But their conclusion also demands examination, and perhaps the best place to start would be to look at the meaning of wealth itself.

The word is derived from 'weal', an archaic term for general well-being usually applied to that of a country or community. Wealth has come to refer to an abundance of material possessions and, while it can now apply to individuals, its original application was also social. The fact that we still refer to the total resources of a country as 'the national wealth' is evidence for the truth that historically all have a claim on national resources, while in contrast the purpose of bourgeois propaganda of which 'wealth creation' forms a part, is to reduce or eliminate all claims on the national wealth not emanating from the business class, to smear or de-legitimise all competing claims.

As the material goods regarded as wealth were derived originally from natural resources of minimal value, those resources needed to be activated, to be 'fertilised by labour', as Bakunin put it, so as to be transformed into more useful products. A pile of stones, for example, has little value until injected with labour to produce a house. Hence the 'stored labour' definition of capital. But what has actually happened in this process? Has wealth been created? Only in a limited or secondary sense. Primarily what's occurred is that resources have been worked on, refined, modified or combined with other resources to produce more useful items. Useful for what? As economics is defined as the study of the production, distribution and consumption of goods, surely the starting point is production and distribution for survival, after which consumption for varying levels of comfort becomes the point of the exercise. No sensible person would deny the legitimacy of this. Why should we chop wood and carry water when solar energy technology can provide us with water pressure and a hot shower?

The process loses its legitimacy when an individual's comfort levels have been achieved and future levels assured (illusory though this may be,) yet the accumulation of useful items continues. Continued accumulation in a world of finite resources can never be justified, for this must take the form of hoarding of resources to which others have a legitimate claim. Defenders of the system will protest that the money mechanism eliminates the hoarding of useful items, that useful items are exchanged for and stored in a form which circulates through the economy providing benefits for all, in particular facilitating the activities of wealth creators. What they don't admit is that this circulation takes the form of a 'V', with the greatest volume and activity at the top among the already wealthy and with little circulation at the base, the base being the only point of access for much of the world's population.

An examination of the nature of the goods we produce and use might seem a pointless exercise, an unnecessary fuss about something that we can safely take for granted, yet it's of the utmost significance, so significant in fact that Marx began his great work *Capital* with just such a study, and admitted that the matter was so complex that these chapters of the book were the most difficult to read. Yet Marx made what appears to be a remarkable oversight in the second paragraph of the opening chapter. He began by stating that the wealth of a capitalist society is presented as an accumulation of commodities, but because this is comprised of single commodities, 'our investigation must begin with the analysis of a commodity.' He went on,

> A commodity is…an object outside us that by its properties satisfies human wants of some sort or another. *The nature of such wants, whether for instance they spring from the stomach or the fancy makes no difference.* (Emphasis added.)

Of course there was no oversight, Marx is referring to the situation as it exists in a capitalist society, and the assumption he brought to light, that all wants have equal validity is so outrageous, so absurd that even the 'mainstream' economist J.K. Galbraith felt moved to criticise an economic structure in which the desire of one person for yet another luxury is given the same status as the need of a hungry person for a meal. But as far as I know Galbraith went no further than this, perhaps realising that further analysis would lead to the conclusion that an economic system based on such irrationality could not and should not be tolerated. For it *should* not be tolerated.

Let's step back from economics for just a moment. In normal daily activities as passengers board a bus, for example, do we assume that those that are aged or infirm have no greater right to seating than others? Of course not; customary attitudes demand that the disadvantaged have greater rights in certain circumstances, while those who fail to respect that expectation are held in contempt by the community. Why should civilised standards not apply in our economic life? Why should those who undermine civilised standards in economic life not be held in contempt also?

Let's return to our discussion of the usefulness of goods. Take the case of those who have transformed natural resources sufficiently to achieve survival. They find they have the capacity for further production, so they quite rightly progress to varying levels of comfort and to cultural pursuits. Surely at this point the sensible, the rational aims of economic activity as defined have been achieved. Further accumulation beyond this point requires justification for we are about to move beyond a process that is sane, that is civilised in the sense of being generally non-exploitative of the world's resources and of other people. Using the money system for further accumulation beyond a reasonable level of comfort is surely indicative of a character deficiency akin to psychosis. What's the point? How can we go beyond comfort? The two most publicised justifications, presented with virtually no criticism, are the pursuit of power or influence and conspicuous consumption. Both of which are plainly manifestations of a profound character deficiency that cannot withstand scrutiny, so the auxiliary forces are brought in. 'We need economic growth' we are told. Why? The drive for economic growth as an end in itself is no more than a modern version of the imperial urge, or expansionism as a means of domination. So we are told we need to compete. Again why? To pander to other people's irrational fears, to allow others the luxury of wallowing in their sickly mistaken perception of what constitutes self-worth? As William Morris pointed out, competition is no more than veiled warfare, and at best ends in wreckage and frustration.

Marx pointed out that from an economic view goods have two values, a use value and an exchange value. It's worth noting that in his essay 'On the Concept of Social Value' the extremely intelligent and articulate Joseph Schumpeter, who studied Marx closely, could only find the existence of exchange value, a great example of the blinkered approach taken by mainstream economists to this fundamental issue. In the same piece he attempted to sweep aside Marx's analysis of surplus value, without actually giving credit to Marx by mentioning him of course, by claiming that in the exchange process no one at all receives full value, as though that somehow validates the inequities of the system and puts to an end the bleating of a troublesome proletariat.

Marx also pointed out that focusing on the exchange value (profit) led to the inevitable immiseration of not only the workforce, but also the profit class. In both cases he was referring to a spiritual misery, a spiritual poverty, even though the process and outcome is different for each. This misery of outlook and self-perception, this poverty of ideals and vision is nowhere more obvious than in the endless mindless search for luxury goods and services, and the payment of obscene sums for items the desirability of which can only be based on fetishism. Consumption, that activity raised to the role of holy ritual by modern economics, that role beyond criticism, no longer serves the cause of survival and comfort, it's been given the function of a drug; it allows its participants to avoid confronting the pointlessness of their existence, the poverty of their inner life.

The misery of the dominant class can also be seen in their rejection of the accepted definition of economics itself. Instead of seeing economics as the study of production distribution and consumption, in other words the study of how we use nature's bounty, they prefer to view it as the study of scarcity. They live in fear. This fear controls them and drives them. Even conspicuous consumption is driven by fear, as it's justified by the unspoken assumption that some have a greater right to the resources of the world than others, an assumption given credence by John Locke, who argued that although resources are common property, we are all entitled to take from the common estate for our exclusive use and, further, that the consent of others is not necessary because, wait for it, people will starve while waiting for others to consent. That's it. That's liberal ethics in a nutshell, a pseudo-philosophy based on fear and uncertainty that creates a world in its own image, but it's important to note that the first liberal thinkers did not dispute the common ownership of natural resources.

It's also important to note that the modern interpretation of mutual obligation (the alleged obligation of those who have nothing to enter into bondage in return for handouts from the wealthy), is a denial of this foundation principle of common ownership. Mutual obligation, a simple and admirable concept fundamental to our view of justice, a concept lodged deep in the consciousness of humanity, has been hijacked, has had the humanity squeezed out of it and now in its modern liberal form is no more than an attempt to deflect attention from the theft behind the amassing of wealth, an attempt to defuse and confuse the legitimate entitlement of all to a share in prosperity, by branding as unworthy those unable to access their fair share. But as it's impossible for an individual to amass great wealth without the assistance of others (evidence again for the social nature of wealth), others who were unpaid or underpaid for their contribution, then the assumption of a right of unbridled accumulation or consumption is invalid.

And of course once these rugged individualists have appropriated their ill-gotten gains, they then bleed the State dry by extorting ongoing subsidy and protection to ensure that the process is endless. As Noam Chomsky put it in *Year 501 – The Conquest Continues,*

> 'Import substitution through state intervention is the only way anyone's ever figured out how to industrialise,' development economist Lance Taylor observes: 'In the long run there are no laissez-faire transitions to modern economic growth. The state has always intervened to create a capitalist class, and then the State has to worry about being taken over by the capitalist class, but the State has always been there.' Furthermore, state power has regularly been invoked by investors and entrepreneurs to protect them from destructive market forces, to secure resources, markets and opportunities for investment, and in general to safeguard and extend their profits and power.

Which is why they mythologise the process, why they deny the history of economic development and create their own reality; their class-based fantasy. Those who use the phrase wealth creation use the word 'wealth' in its original whole-of-society context; for they imply that this process is for the general good. They know that the world's resources are public property. They know that if the public demands access to those resources they cannot be denied. They know that for their dominant role and excessive consumption to continue the public must be lulled into accepting what is no more than a creation myth, a distortion of reality, for in the final analysis, wealth is created not by particular individuals or a particular class but by society. It is a public good to which all should have access and to which, in a decent and moral society, no one should have unlimited access.

Afternote

By redefining economics as the study of scarcity, it immediately becomes the study of the maximisation of economic security, a search for the unattainable, for a chimera, an illusion, a wild imaginary ideal more closely aligned to insanity than reality. That insanity is clearly seen in the foundation articles of liberalism that competition will bring benefits to all and that free market democracy is so far above criticism that it must and will be imposed by force on those who resist it. Such thinking has obvious major flaws, but one perhaps a little less obvious is that we do not gain security by making the lives of others more dangerous or more difficult; quite the opposite. Yet that is what is practised when economics is the study of scarcity; for to put it in its crudest terms, economics then becomes the creed of 'get what you can while you can' – in other words, how to maximise your enemies. Now if we do not gain security by making the lives of others more dangerous and difficult, then the corollary of that is that we can gain security by making the lives of others less dangerous and difficult, in short, by cooperation. A realistic and productive view of economics, therefore, is that it should be the study of the maximisation of the benefits of cooperative behaviour and of the structures that facilitate such behaviour.

Shall We Eat the Cabin Boy?
An examination of liberal ethics

Those hardy souls who delve into the murky origins of free market philosophy soon realise that modern economic policy is based largely on the classical economics that grew out of the Industrial Revolution in Britain; they realise that classical economics was developed as a propaganda weapon in the class war brought on by industrial upheaval, and that Darwin's theory of evolution was also used in this war, to give the appearance of scientific backing to an emerging economic framework that was resisted bitterly by working people at the time. Certain scientists have even suggested that accepted assumptions about evolution have more to do with the social attitudes and conditions that prevailed in Victorian Britain than with impartial science.[1]

But what is not so apparent to the researcher is that the propagandists of social theory concentrated then, and still do today, on Darwin's *Origin of Species*, deliberately side-stepping his later work *The Descent of Man*, in which he clearly demonstrated that mankind's social instincts are primary and individual instincts secondary, thereby destroying the keystone of classical economics and, consequently, modern economic dogma. So it was not Darwin's work that was unbalanced; it was the propagandists who attached themselves to him, and their work, that were a natural consequence of British attitudes of the day.

The Industrial Revolution flowed from a revolution in free thought including scientific enquiry that took place across Europe, and it was at this time that the class warriors of the bourgeoisie anticipated the crucial role that science could play in facilitating their narrow preferences for social development. So began a process of interpreting new findings and channelling enquiry to achieve class-based outcomes that continues today. (For example, in the fields of genetic engineering of crops, repeated attempts to revive eugenics, space exploration for military ends, medical research for profit, sham environmentalism funded by corporate polluters. The list is endless.) Their campaign to have natural selection based solely on competition between unequal individuals has been a success story of staggering proportions, as they were resisted from the outset by opposing views based on superior science.

Peter Kropotkin, a Russian geographer, became alarmed at the shabby science that was promoted by 'Darwin's bulldog', Thomas Huxley, and began publishing a series of rebuttals that were eventually put together in book form under the title *Mutual Aid – A Factor in Evolution*. Kropotkin acknowledged the significance of competition in evolutionary change, but he presented a comprehensive history of the natural and human world that showed mutual aid and sociality to have been a greater factor in survival, and in our moral outlook,[2] than the competition being promoted in isolation by Darwin's bulldogs. *Mutual Aid* is fascinating and highly readable.

Though Kropotkin was a saintly character from all accounts, the task of sidelining his work was possibly made easier by his reputation as a philosopher of anarchism, but the scientific basis of his work should not be dismissed lightly as he has been supported indirectly and directly in recent times by two eminent anthropologists. Richard Leakey has suggested that sharing of food among early humans was the foundation of our ideas on justice, while Stephen Jay Gould has given this support to *Mutual Aid*:

> As a young man, long before his conversion to political radicalism, Kropotkin spent five years in Siberia (1862–1866) just after Darwin published the *Origin of Species*... He observed a sparsely populated world, swept with frequent catastrophes that threatened the few species able to find a place in such bleakness. As a potential disciple of Darwin, he looked for competition, but rarely found any. Instead, he continually observed the benefits of mutual aid... What can we make of Kropotkin's argument today, and that of the entire Russian

school represented by him? Were they just victims of cultural hope and intellectual conservatism? I don't think so. In fact, I would hold that Kropotkin's basic argument is correct.

Kropotkin continued developing this theme of mutual aid in a collection of notes on the history and development of justice, ethics and morality, which were put in book form after his death under the title *Ethics*. He summarised his findings thus: 'without equity there is no justice, without justice, no morality'. The connection he made between mutual aid and morality is simple yet profound: that this was the starting point of morality because it was mutual aid that allowed the earliest human communities to survive and flourish, that actions by individuals in their personal interests that upset the harmony provided by mutual aid were a danger to the community and consequently regarded as unjust or immoral. From the outset, collective welfare took precedence over individual welfare and, when you think about it, that's what morality is all about. After all, the term is derived from 'mores', being social rules, etiquette or inhibitions. Whether we are considering collective harm, as for example with company fraud, or individual harm as with murder, the catch cry is always 'The community must be protected.'[3]

It was from *Ethics* that another factor emerged that allowed Kropotkin's work to be sidelined. He gave evidence that the rudiments of morality existed in other forms of life prior to the emergence of humans. In that era of widespread notions of racial and cultural superiority, such a suggestion would have been intolerable (the English gentry had trouble accepting that their workers felt the same emotions as the upper classes.) and probably not much has changed today. You won't find too many references to Kropotkin in discussions of ethics, yet Thomas Hobbes (1588–1679), who was no more than a myth-maker for the bourgeoisie, is regularly trotted out as a thinker of substance. His most famous argument, that the lives of the earliest humans were 'poor, solitary, nasty, brutal and short', and that the natural state of mankind is one of perpetual strife, with each man at war with every other man, is an appalling fabrication. As this was the foundation of Hobbes's philosophy, his entire work should have been dismissed at once, but he wrote just as the English middle class were hitting their straps, and those desperate for moral justification are rarely fussy as to detail.[4]

Once John Locke had tinkered here, tinkered there, and taken the monarchy out of Hobbesism, Hobbes was assured of his place in the liberal pantheon.[5] (That's 'liberal' as in 'economic individualism', not the almost meaningless US usage.) His beliefs that now flow through every liberal writer from Locke to Robert Nozick became the basis of free market theory and liberal policy, yet they are littered with superficial nonsense. For example, as an individualist Hobbes believed that one is morally justified in doing whatever is necessary to save one's own life, that self-preservation is unconditionally morally permissible. James MacAdam of the Philosophy Department, Trent University, Ontario, has applied this thinking to the case of The Queen v. Dudley and Stephens (1884), which involved two seamen, who after several days adrift in a lifeboat with no food and no prospect of rescue, killed and ate the cabin boy. They offered the defence of necessity, and according to MacAdam, Hobbes would agree.

But, MacAdam asks, if self-preservation is morally right, is self-sacrifice to save another morally wrong? Though this is typical of the illogicalities on which liberal theory is based, MacAdam was unable to criticise Hobbes; instead he found that this belief leads to a significant concept that 'explains the enduring importance of Hobbes' philosophy'. MacAdam's argument is that

> without security of life, then liberty, equality, justice etc cannot exist... the other philosophers claim moral superiority for their principles, but Hobbes can claim logical priority for his as without his the others cannot apply.

He continued,

> Hobbes' position is: 'all the duties of rulers are contained in this one sentence; the safety of the people is the supreme law'.

Enduring philosophical importance? Hobbes merely stated the obvious. Furthermore, this truism has been eagerly embraced by every tyrant and warmonger in history. John Howard even used it to make criminals of asylum seekers.

The dangerous superficiality of Hobbes's work can also be seen in his view that 'The origin of all society is to be found in the mutual fear of all its members' because 'All in their natural condition are possessed of the will to injure others.' This led him to conclude that civil society is comprised of people coming together uneasily, suspicious of each other's motives, under a strong leader for mutual protection, that leader requiring in return, unquestioning obedience. From this Hegel made the suggestion, subsequently adopted by US strategists, that civil society is 'the realm in which men pursue their self-interest and treat others as a means to their ends'.[6]

Put these beliefs together and it's not hard to see why authoritarianism is the natural endgame of liberalism. An ideology based on individualism must by its very nature generate little if any social cohesion, and will most likely undermine social concepts and institutions. (as in the urge to privatise public utilities). Its resulting system, in order to prevent splintering, must be authoritarian, and because liberals have expanded their fear and suspicion into the global arena, their system will be militaristic and aggressive as we see today.

These are not simply criticisms from an outsider with an axe to grind, but the inevitable consequences of their own explanations of themselves and of their perception of the world. We should not accept for a moment their pious claims that respect for diversity and human dignity are the hallmarks of liberalism. Liberals despise, fear and oppose, often with brutal force, any form of self-determination which actually empowers people by preventing elite control of economic affairs. Liberalism brooks no rivals despite its alleged devotion to the ideal of competition, and its true regard for diversity can be seen in the periodic purging of progressives by the Liberal Party in Australia.

Let's be clear on some crucial points. Hobbes believed that society is built on fear because each individual has base motives and acts lawfully only through fear of legal penalties. This erroneous belief permeates liberal thought. Ethical principles, not fear, are actually the essence of social life. As we interact with others in our daily life, it's ethical standards that provide us with the guidelines for a sociality that is mutually agreeable and productive. Social life can exist without fear but it cannot exist without ethics. Liberalism has side-stepped history and logic, making legal principles the foundation of civil society. Whenever the alleged virtues of liberalism are trumpeted to the world, it's not ethics or decency and fairness that get a mention, it's 'the rule of law' and 'property rights'.

We can conclude therefore that there is no ethical basis to liberal thought, there is no liberal ethos. The really sad fact, however, is that Hobbes's dismal view of society, sick and twisted though it was, has become a self-fulfilling prophecy. The base, the suspicious and the fearful, have a grip on power and are shaping the world in their own image. This is not mere rhetoric. Their unrelenting campaign against unionism is evidence not only of an acceptance of Hobbes's false view of historical man, but of a wish and a striving for Hobbesian man. If liberals were genuine in their concern for the alleged savagery of ordinary people, they would see unionism as an evolutionary advance towards a state of harmony. Instead they see unionism as a threat to their class interests and prefer to see collective action eliminated and society accordingly weakened to preserve narrow sectional interests. The liberal ideal is not one of harmonious development and social evolution, of voluntary association and mutual aid of the kind unions and other less formal groupings can give; their ideal is a fragmented society managed by an all-powerful state.

Those doubting Hobbes's malign influence on contemporary affairs should consider the case of Jeanne Kirkpatrick, Ronald Reagan's ambassador to the UN, who amazingly quoted Hobbes, dead for three hundred years, in defence of the Salvadorean junta responsible for the murder of three US nuns and a lay worker. Closer to home and more telling still, check out a charming little volume titled *Liberal Thinking*, written by Senator Chris Puplick in 1980 in association with the Liberal Federal Executive Philosophy Sub-Committee no less. Not only is Hobbes's view of society rehashed and presented as a work in progress, but they managed to write an entire book on liberal philosophy without referring once to its originators. This was no accident. Readers were informed with stunning condescension and deceit that

> Political philosophies tend to go hand in hand with ethical theories. Historically however, liberalism has been associated with a diversity of such theories. It would, accordingly, be unrewarding to try here to discover the ethical framework in which liberalism should be placed.

I'll bet it would. They brazenly continued,

> It would also be unrewarding here to delve too deeply into the philosophical validity of various ethical theories.

Intellectual rigour at its best. But this was not their only cover-up. The same contempt for the very same truth shown by Thomas Huxley when he concealed in a footnote to an essay the impact of mutual aid on evolution,[7] while refusing to recant on the primacy of personal instincts is present throughout *Liberal Thinking*, as the authors tried to reconcile the social sentiments of the public with the anti-social, and therefore immoral, realities of individualism. Mind you, we must feel for them just a little. It can't be easy presenting yourself to the world as a collective of individualists.

But construction of the liberal edifice did not end with Hobbes. It needed just one more outrageous assertion to give us liberalism in its modern form. It was John Locke (1632–1704) who stated that man had the right to 'Preserve his Property, that is, his Life, Liberty, and Estate'. Curiously, every schoolchild knows that property is tangible, and that property is so far removed from life and liberty that it's almost without value in comparison. But truth and honesty are impediments to profit, and so Locke's inanity was hailed as a philosophical breakthrough by delighted liberals the world over, who reasoned that if everything of value was now property, then everything of value was a commodity to be bought and sold.[8] So was built the liberal dream, a fantasy world in which property is sacred, protected by penalties of the same order as those applying to crimes against life and liberty. The nightmare world of chaos and anguish that we see about us is to a very large extent a victory, the realisation of the liberal dream.

Notes

1. In particular, Dr Mae-wan Ho, Director of the British-based Institute of Science in Society.

2. Huxley and others attempted to derive an ethical framework from the triumph of the strong over the weak. See note 7.

3. The liberal belief that society is an arrangement designed to protect individuals from each other contains an inherent contradiction. Once a collective has been formed, for whatever reason, there clearly exists a tacit acknowledgement that individual rights have been surrendered in favour of collective rights, yet liberals cling to the contradiction that the primary purpose of society is the protection of individual rights. Logic demands that individual rights are a secondary consideration, in line with the findings of Darwin, Kropotkin and others, that social instincts are primary and individual instincts secondary. Liberals cannot see, or refuse to admit, that membership of a collective involves an automatic empowering of the individual.

4. There's a delightful little reference in Kropotkin's *Ethics* to his public battle with Huxley that goes, 'Huxley, whom I had to remind, when he began developing ideas worthy of Hobbes, that the appearance of societies on earth preceded the appearance of man.' And another: 'This brilliant evolutionist, who was so successful in spreading Darwin's teaching of the gradual development of organic forms on the earth, proved quite incapable of following his great teacher in the realm of moral thought.'

5. Hobbes is rarely quoted by present-day liberal apologists as his arguments are so easily refuted, but one significant figure with no such qualms was Francis Fukuyama, who in his *End of History and The Last Man* proudly paired Hobbes and Locke repeatedly as the founding fathers of liberal thought.

6. The West's invasion of Iraq is just one more instance of military intervention designed in part to establish the Hobbes–Hegel version of democracy, much of the history of the last few centuries being concerned with this particular impulse and efforts to resist it. The current antagonism of the US towards Venezuelan president Hugo Chavez is due to Chavez laying the foundations of

a regional system of cooperation and fair trading, concepts inconsistent with the preferred arrangement of perpetual strife and the domination of the weak by the powerful. But such truths need concealment, concealment so regular it becomes a pattern. The so-called 'history wars' recently waged in Australia and the USA were a desperate attempt by the bourgeoisie to regain control of the presentation of history, particularly to young impressionable minds, as no trace of ignoble motives or actions in the pursuit of power are permissible, the worst allowable criticism being blunders committed with noble intent, a justification frequently cited, for example, in defence of the Stolen Generations tragedy, the invasion of Vietnam etc.

7. 1893, *Collected Essays*, 'Evolution and Ethics', note 20.

8. Locke and Hobbes had a profound influence on the framers of the US Constitution, the effects of which are still being played out on the world stage today.

Francis Fukuyama
and the Myths of Liberal Democracy

His 1992 book *The End of History and The Last Man* earned Francis Fukuyama wealth and international acclaim. The book was generally well received in Australia (particularly among adherents of the political Third Way) and in his native USA, but the reception in Britain verged on the rapturous. There the author was referred to as the man who 'shook the world', 'one of the few enduring public intellectuals' and 'the thinking man's thinking man'. All this for a self-interested serving of psycho-babble outstanding only for its transparent shallowness.

The conclusion Fukuyama drew from his 'universal history' was that today's liberal democracies represent the pinnacle of human social achievement and that the present dominance of liberalism is evidence that we are witnessing the last days of social evolution. Hence the title.

One of the points hammered repeatedly was that the superiority of liberal democracy is proved by the fact that no modern liberal democracies have ever gone to war against each other. Now this is a powerful argument, made more powerful by the beauty of its simplicity. We can almost sense the Hand of God at work here; mankind's long-awaited compliance with His Eternal Plan. If Fukuyama's argument is a demonstrable fact, and it would seem to be simple to prove or disprove, it gives credibility to his assertion and something of a justification for the less savoury aspects of capitalism.

Of course one objection to this line of thinking springs quickly to mind – that is, the long-established pattern of US destabilisation and overthrow of democratically elected governments, but this is just as quickly rebutted by Fukuyama's extremely clever proviso that he refers only to liberal (that's economists' code for free market) democracies. Genuine democracies that actually work in the interests of their people are excluded from this grand plan for their failure to serve the mystical market. The possibility that peoples and nations might have the right to determine their own direction is never entertained in the ever-so-liberal mind of Francis Fukuyama.

And this narrow view of democracy shows what a wonderful argument Fukuyama has presented. If market democracy is in fact the pinnacle of human achievement and can guarantee lasting peace, then all of those dirty little wars, those countless tortures, mutilations and murders committed in the interests of US foreign policy, were no more than divinely directed diversions along the petal-strewn path to mankind's crowning glory. No sleepless nights in that lot for the former State Department policy director.

So is he correct in asserting that liberal democracies have never waged war on each other? Not really. The historical record seems to bear him out, but only if we accept that such entities have actually existed. The US, for instance, is most frequently cited as the best example of a market democracy, but is in reality a bastion of protectionism that pays lip service only to the ideals of liberal economics. So an argument can be mounted that true liberal democracy is a figment of a fevered imagination, but for the sake of the discussion let's assume that Fukuyama's ideal is real.

If Fukuyama's democracies have not been waging war on each other, what have they been doing? A glance at the tip of the historical iceberg is interesting.

Alexander Hamilton, one of the US Founding Fathers, described the people as a great beast that has to be controlled. James Madison, one of the framers of the US Constitution, stated that those who control the wealth must control the nation. The founder of free market economics, David Ricardo, stated in his *Law of Wages*, which is still an article of textbook dogma, that 'the natural price of labour is the price necessary to enable the labourer to subsist and to perpetuate his race without increase or diminution.' You will note the clear implication that labour is a mere commodity and that labourers are a race apart whose sole reason for existing is to serve their superiors. Rather like cattle. He gave rise to no doubts or pangs of conscience among today's economic trend-setters with this explanation:

> When the market price of labour is below its natural price, poverty deprives them of necessaries. When the resultant privations have reduced their number, the market price will rise to the natural price.

Charming.

Sir Keith Joseph, who converted the British Conservative Party to market economics, believed that 'sterility, like despotism, is a necessary consequence of the egalitarian ideal in practice.' He believed that the presence of inequality in society was a sign of a healthy society.

Since the success of the Thatcherite revolution, social democratic parties the world over, as well as conservative parties, have been convinced that acceptance of free market philosophy is the only option for sound economic management. Sovereignty has been conceded to the market and therefore necessarily to those in a position to manipulate the market. The interests of the business community, for so long acknowledged as inimical to the social good, have somehow been relocated to a position beyond criticism.

Since the US steel disputes of the 1930s, US corporations, followed by corporations worldwide, have spent billions annually on propaganda designed to tell the public that there is nothing wrong with the system, while deliberately obscuring its actual workings. This strike-breaking tactic was known as the Mohawk Valley Formula and was received in business circles with great excitement for its novelty and potential benefits, but is now so pervasive that it goes unnoticed. As serving the interests of the business community is now accepted as the prime function of government, this project of misinformation now has the blessing of government.

The conclusion is unpleasant but inescapable. Because acceptance of the basic tenets of free market philosophy involves the promotion of inequality, the reason that Fukuyama's democracies have not been at war with each other is because they have been at war with their own citizens. They have been allied (GATT, WTO, IMF and so on) in a struggle to insulate the corporate sector from the threat of real democracy. That may not be the intent in the case of social democratic governments, but it is certainly the inevitable outcome. We are the observers and the victims of an appalling lack of understanding – you cannot embrace the market without declaring war on the people.

Furthermore, others have demonstrated that the suppression of democracy is the whole purpose of 'liberal democracy', but for now it is sufficient to point out that the current dominance of an ideology dedicated to serving a minority is hardly a justification for declaring the end of history.

Defending Society from Attacks by the State

A Radio National *Late Night Live* program broadcast in mid-October 2004 featured a British scientist discussing the false assumptions that lie behind genetic engineering, in particular the production of genetically modified food crops. It seems that there is increasing evidence that the assumption made upon the discovery of DNA, that DNA influences organic processes by a linear chain of command similar to that which exists in a corporation or government, is not the case. Increasing numbers of scientists are coming to the conclusion that cellular organic processes are better described as ecological, in that they come about by a network of interdependent connections and communications rather like the processes that take place in nature at the level of the organism. They do not occur through a one-step process of cause and effect; they come about after a host of influences play a role. It is increasingly understood therefore that the rather brutal exercise of inserting foreign DNA into a cell could be counter-productive or even unsafe, because the foreign matter does not understand the 'language' of the host, cannot participate in its rhythms of life. The modified organism can then be unstable. (I realise that the analogy taking shape here could be used as an argument against asylum seekers, but that would be simplistic and false. The history of human advancement is largely the history of migrations. Insular societies stagnate.)

Our history has been plagued by false assumptions, notably in the field of pure science, but to no less an extent in the social sciences. It's almost universally assumed for example that the State is the official embodiment of society, that the State is representative of society and serves its needs. But is that the case? The parallel between the organic processes described above and social processes is a telling one. Society functions in an ecological manner, by a network of communications and influences that induce outcomes that are impossible to predict.

The state, on the other hand, operates through a hierarchical chain of command. It often has the mind-set of the scientist who inserts foreign DNA into a cell, acting in an authoritarian manner and making somewhat brutal decisions.

This might be defended on the grounds that these decisions are made for the good of the majority, but is that always the case?

I doubt if there was a single member of even the Coalition government, let alone the general public, who believed in the days after the 11 September 2001 attacks that an invasion of Iraq would be a reasonable response. After a massive public relations exercise emanating from the US, the majority of Australians still did not believe an invasion reasonable, yet it went ahead with our government's support. A foreign concept was inserted into our national affairs. (I know we have a history of willing participation in ill-considered foreign adventures, but in this case even our subservient media displayed bewildered dissent in the early stages, until they were reminded of their allotted role in a market democracy.)

Did this insertion serve society or did it destabilise the organism as in the DNA analogy? We are now participating in state terrorism on a huge scale, assisting in the killing of thousands of civilians, helping to undermine the Geneva Conventions and international law in general, decimating a state half a world away, and making ourselves targets for retaliatory terrorism. Serving our interests? Hardly. Destabilised? Surely. Our participation in a war that we rejected is obviously a case of the State serving a need other than ours. That need must be considered by the State to be more important than our need. Whose need can it be?

Any number of reasons can be offered for the US decision to invade Iraq, but the reason for our compliance is a different question altogether. It has been noted that many of the puzzling and immoral decisions made in national and world affairs can be put down to an habitual acquiescence to the wishes of the powerful. But in the absence of a credible or sustainable retaliation by the US for non-compliance by Australia, and the level of initial domestic risk for the Coalition associated with compliance, that possibility seems to be ruled out. The most likely option left is that Howard acted to promote class interests. He put class interests ahead of the national interest. That view is supported by his later decision to refuse a request by the UN to send more troops to Iraq as support for UN personnel. The UN is not noted for being representative of bourgeois values. Its interests do not correspond with Howard's interests, hence the refusal. The view that this was a war by and for bourgeois interests is also supported by what we have actually witnessed in Iraq. We've seen the destruction of a primitive socialist state, which for all its many faults could boast the highest living standards in the region. Higher than in many areas of the US itself, and certainly higher than that in US domains. We've seen its replacement by a hand-picked business-based oligarchy that will see its economy totally privatised, bereft of public assets, its only asset of significance locked into contractual arrangements with the West that will ensure an outflow of wealth for years to come. This in turn will ensure that Iraq remains a source of instability for years to come, but that will be considered irrelevant as bourgeois interests will have been served – profits for Western companies, justification for an on-going military presence, and the removal of a rival political model to which others in the region might aspire.

When all of the 'rational' reasons for our participation in barbarity evaporated on close inspection, our compliance was ensured by appeals to the irrational aspects of patriotism. Mikhail Bakunin made a comment on this very matter of patriotism in 1869, which is as perceptive and relevant today:

> The very existence of the State demands that there be some privileged class vitally interested in maintaining that existence. And it is precisely the group interests of that class that are called patriotism.

That seems a little extreme until we recall something of the history behind the origins of the modern form of the State. Joseph Schumpeter, no admirer of Bakunin, supported the first of Bakunin's assertions with this definition:

The State is the product of the clashes and compromises that took place between the feudal lords and the bourgeoisie.

In other words, there was no democratic or whole-of-society outlook involved in the origins of the nation-state. It was a compromise between rival classes of elites. And the second of Bakunin's assertions has been amply demonstrated by the Howard government.

Any action that destabilises or endangers society is an attack on society. The most reasonable action we can take to protect ourselves from attack is to contribute to, strengthen, enhance and create anew those ecological bonds, connections and interdependencies, local and global, that differentiate us from hierarchical structures, and which ultimately are far more stable, enduring, productive, progressive and rewarding.

It's All About Property, Right?

But just what is property? That was the question asked by Pierre-Joseph Proudhon in 1840. His answer? A thunderous 'Property is theft'. What could have prompted such an outburst? Let's look at some aspects of the question considered by Proudhon and some that were not.

When the bourgeoisie began their three and a half century rise to political ascendency the central plank of their program was the alleged right to acquire, possess and trade property and commodities of any kind. Once that concept had gained acceptance, all that remained was to reduce or eliminate any restraints or limits that might be placed on that right by rulers or legislatures. Of course people had always possessed and traded goods, so what was it that set the bourgeoisie on this course, what set them apart from previous entrepreneurial groups?

John Locke, whose influence on bourgeois thinking has been immeasurable, stated the generally accepted position that God gave the world to mankind 'in common to use for its preservation', but then had to attempt the torturous exercise of justifying the appropriation of resources from the common store for exclusive use by individuals.

J.S. Mill, also a powerful influence on liberal thought, although writing a century and a half after Locke, also took it as given that resources were common to all, showing that the notion was widespread and long-lived. However, Mill rejected private property accumulation based on what the bourgeoisie were now calling 'natural property rights' (in reality unnatural rights) sensibly believing that such rights should be assessed in terms of their overall social utility, but fearing the limits to personal freedom that he assumed would accrue under socialism he opted for private property and capitalism. (Although an outstanding intellectual, Mill apparently overlooked the possibility of a libertarian strain of socialism.) Significantly, a further reason for this decision was his astounding claim in *Political Economy* Volume 2 that private property had not been given a fair trial in any country, a clear indication that modern attitudes to property relations are a relatively recent development. It's of great significance therefore that in Mill's era the rising bourgeoisie were transforming traditional views as to the nature of property, removing it from its social context into one entirely class-based. Property accumulation is therefore not the natural harmonious activity central to human evolution that its proponents would have us believe. Any doubts Mill had as to alleged natural rights to property have been ignored by the liberal mainstream along with his conversion in later years to socialism.

T.H. Green took over Mill's position as the 'schoolmaster of British liberalism' and accepted then transformed Locke's concept of the common store into a common good which again was entirely class-based, that is, a common freedom for 'the pursuit of self-realisation' by the given members of a society. In other words, a common freedom to enrich oneself from the common store. Versions of this are still floated by liberal apologists today. The idea is class-based as it ignores the reality that those born with a head start in life have greater freedom than others. He justified inequalities of property as mere indications of varying tastes and talents, denied that the accumulation of property within capitalist relations implied by necessity the impoverishment of the wage-earning class, and falsely contended that in an ideal free market property would become available to all. His views on land ownership are instructive. Rights to non-renewable resources such as land depended on rendering them 'more serviceable to society as a whole than if they were held in common', 'for the capital gained by one is not taken from another if it is compensated by the acquisition of other wealth on the part of those extruded from the soil', a wonderful piece of self-serving bourgeois sophistry if ever there was one, for he conceded or implied that social rights are primary, but the subsequent development of liberal thought on the matter allowed for no right by society to oversee or intervene if the resulting private land use was seen to be inadequate for society's needs or if the wealth enjoyed by 'those extruded' was found to be less than compensatory.

It was by falsehoods and fabrications such as these that liberalism laid the foundations for the political and economic outlook that dominates the globe today, and naturally enough there was a reaction at the time by critics who could see behind the rhetoric to the unattractive reality beyond. One of the most notable of these critics was Proudhon. He did not dismiss the concept of private property entirely despite his declaration that property is theft; instead he held to the traditional view of property, believing that all had a right to own personal items such as house, land and tools of trade. His protest was aimed at the private ownership of the means of mass production – that is, large land holdings, industrial plant and so on – and the exploitation of labour that such property necessarily entailed. In short, he saw that the newly distorted concept of property involved theft from society in the appropriation and theft from the workforce in the utilisation. It's less well-known that in his famous tract 'What Is Property?' Proudhon also declared that 'Property is freedom'. By this he meant that the personal assets of people, their homes, workshops, tools of trade, were the means by which they could resist being overwhelmed by the demands of the propertied class and the coercive powers of so-called representative democracy. He believed that larger industrial enterprises should be in the hands of cooperatives rather than individuals or corporations, and that individual property accumulation should be limited to levels that could comfortably be utilised or made productive by the individual's own hands.

Curiously, the path of British liberalism took an almost surreal turn some time later under the influence of L.T. Hobhouse. Hobhouse was a liberal in the tradition of Mill, having a healthy scepticism in regard to alleged natural rights to property, but he sounded more like a Proudhonian than a liberal on the subject when he wrote in 1911,

That there are rights to property we all admit. Is there not (as well) a general right TO property? Is there not something radically wrong with an economic system under which…vast inequalities are perpetuated? Ought we to acquiesce in a condition in which the great majority are born to nothing except what they can earn, while some are born to more than the social value of any individual of whatever merit?

Clearly the deceit practiced by liberalism on the public had become so obvious and appalling that even some liberals were concerned. The wealth-creating resources that all sectors had conceded belonged originally to society, had been appropriated by the private sector on the basis of a promised compensatory social benefit, a benefit that now proved to be illusory.

Hobhouse deflated another favourite claim of the business sector, yet another claim still circulating today, the right of entrepreneurs to the exclusive enjoyment of profits.

The prosperous businessman who thinks he has made his fortune entirely by self-help does not pause to consider what single step he could have taken on the road to success but for the ordered tranquillity which has made commercial development possible, the security by road, rail and sea, the masses of skilled labour, and the sum of intelligence which civilisation has placed at his disposal, the very demand for goods which he produces that the progress of the world has created, the inventions he uses as a matter of course that have been built up by the collective effort of generations…as it is society that maintains and guarantees his possessions, so also it is society that is an indispensable partner in its original creation.

He concluded, 'The basis of property is social.'

This shows that with the passage of time the fact that property was once considered a common resource had been forgotten; Hobhouse had to use logic to demonstrate his point rather than historical references. There will be many who claim today that such a belief never enjoyed general acceptance, but they choose to forget the history of liberal thought. One of the justifications used by the bourgeoisie for their taking control of the common store was their accurate description of previous feudal and aristocratic rights as being illegitimate, won from the people by theft and force. The aristocracy had used the very same pretext now being used by the bourgeoisie; an alleged superior ability to manage the common estate. Once ensconced, they turned managerial rights into total rights, a path their successors have attempted to follow.

The reaction to this middle-class property grab was so widespread throughout society that liberalism was forced to give ground, but not forced to abandon its base. The bourgeoisie were saved by a fetish, the commodity fetish described by Marx which infected the whole of society and could only be satisfied, or so it was believed, by capitalist modes of production. So to preserve the newly acquired need to consume, with all the illusions of achievement and satisfaction that this entailed, illegitimate rights to unlimited property accumulation and the commodity view of labour were retained, while in return taxation was used to extract a measure of compensation for society.

With the business sector now relentlessly chipping away at the legitimacy of taxation as a form of rent paid to society for the right to unlimited profit, the future looks bleak. There are a few encouraging signs, however. In the documentary *The Corporation*, the principal company owner interviewed told of his dismay at learning of the staggering level of resources used to manufacture his particular product. He realised instinctively that he was taking unreasonably from a global base belonging to all. This demonstrates the artificiality of alleged 'natural rights' to acquire property. It is a manufactured right. Our instincts tell us that the true, the only, natural right lies with society and the only means by which private property rights can have legitimacy is by way of a partial right granted by the community under agreed conditions. Many customs and attitudes now current are based, perhaps unconsciously, on a tacit recognition of this reality. We expect mining companies, for example, to pay royalties on extracted wealth and to enter into site regeneration agreements. The environmental and conservation movements certainly operate on the basis of partial property rights by attempting to put limits on certain activities regardless of the nature of property title, though I'm not sure they express the issue in terms of property relations. Building codes and other regulatory frameworks are all evidence of an acceptance of the primary role of society in determining property rights. Private property as an inalienable right is an illusion, a myth, a class-based fantasy.

Another encouraging sign was displayed in *Voice* 17. Tim Metcalf's interview with participants in the Mumbulla Bioregion project was a delight to read. If I can summarise the thrust of the project, those involved see a sustainable future as one based on the sharing of resources and property within a manageable geographical area. As regional sustainability is the prime criterion, the project is the precise opposite of the present economic system based on the mindless global accumulation of property with no regard for cultural and environmental values. Not only can the participants see the way forward, they've taken the steps to making the potential a reality. All who take part will be materially, culturally and spiritually enriched.

The virtual bio-region concept is consistent with the social and economic structure advocated by Proudhon, that is, a federation of voluntary associations held together at all levels by mutual aid, benefit and respect, all of which are underpinned by a sense of justice that he believed is innate to humanity. The bio-region concept is revolutionary, and compatible with Proudhon's belief that

> The task for revolutionaries, therefore, is not to overthrow the existing political order but to transform the economic basis of society.

But the time for handling the business sector with kid gloves is long gone. They've proved themselves incapable of managing the resources with which they were entrusted by society in simpler times. We have two options, one modest, one less so, if we are to achieve sustainable development. We must re-assert the primary rights of society, enforce accounting procedures that include the environmental and social costs of business activities and regulate and tax accordingly. If that fails or is resisted the concept of private property rights as they now exist must be abolished. That seems extreme, but consider this. We live in an era of global warming, unprecedented rates of species extinction, ceaseless clearing of native forests, and disposal of radioactive wastes into the sea. The list of such crises and crimes is endless, and each alone is a threat to our survival. Together they pose a threat that cannot be ignored, and all stem from the twin addictions of consumerism and property accumulation. As we face this dilemma, Proudhon's apparently outrageous declaration that property is theft seems modest, reasonable, focused, and a worthy rallying cry.

Free Traders Old and New

In their now customary habit of reshaping the world to suit the needs of empire, US officials have in recent years been engaged in an interesting exercise in the Baltic area. At an economic conference titled 'Towards a New Hanseatic League' held in Finland in 1997, the US ambassador to Finland stated that the US would like to oversee the formation of a local free trade zone to return the Baltic region to its former position of wealth and influence, a position that it once enjoyed under the control of the medieval Hanseatic League. (There would be nothing in this arrangement to benefit the US, of course, persistent paranoia concerning containment of Russia does not come into it.) The US Deputy Assistant Secretary of State Ron Asmus, interestingly responsible for the expansion of NATO among other things (note the US linkage of matters economic and military) also spoke at the conference and it is notable that he confessed to having no prior knowledge of the league. So just what was the Hanseatic League?

From the twelfth to the sixteenth centuries, trading guilds based around the Baltic controlled much of Europe's trade and wielded considerable political influence. These trading cooperatives were formed to gain protection from pirates, and from robber barons extorting feudal tolls and levies, kings being unable or unwilling to enforce order. As the benefits of the cooperatives became apparent to the royal houses by way of increased taxes from increased trade, the Hansa (defensive societies, loosely grouped) gained great favour and were granted charters to establish free cities devoted to trade enhancement. These cities then formed a fluid and informal federation known as the Hanseatic League.

The free cities became thriving centres, forces for civilisation, and models for cooperative development. The trading guilds encouraged all other guilds to participate in the life of the city, and as a result the arts flourished, particularly architecture, with all citizens assisting in the building of cathedrals, hospitals and schools. Peaceful development became the norm, with the Hansa preventing war between rival cities. They were prepared to defend their turf, however, and were not afraid to take up arms even against kings who in their opinion were disruptive to trade.

Several factors contributed to the eventual decline of the league. They lacked the internal organisation necessary to survive the rise of the nation state. They attempted to enforce monopolies, rarely a sound practice and one that encourages enemies. But more importantly, they failed to grasp one of the main principles of cooperation and mutualism; the concept must be universal in application or it will not be at all. Two outcomes flowed from this lack of understanding. A class system developed over time whereby the burghers saw themselves as a privileged patrician class, excluding the peasantry from active life in the cities. And the Hansa concentrated their wealth in trade and industry to the neglect and detriment of the agricultural sector. Any political system that fails to see society as an organic whole contains the seeds of its own destruction. These divisions allowed rival alliances to be formed that eventually rendered the Hanseatic League irrelevant.

So if the US is successful in its push for a Baltic free trade zone, will this arrangement bear any resemblance to its medieval counterpart?

None at all.

Because modern free market philosophy is based on self-interest and the cult of the individual, today's free trade agreements contain no provisions for cooperation, or provisions for community advancement. Quite the opposite. Today's free trade agreements do not even concentrate on freedom of trade; they are actually legislative frameworks aimed at protecting corporations from community pressure. The North American Free Trade Agreement, for example, places great emphasis on enforcing a dubious interpretation of intellectual property rights that has been shown to be detrimental to the public good by stifling competition. In other words, the agreement encourages monopolies, one of the outcomes that it was supposedly designed to prevent. Hence the perceived need to protect corporations from a justifiably outraged public.

The contrast with the Hanseatic League could not be greater. Cooperation, mutual aid, and community development were the principles upon which they operated. They developed their own system of justice, maritime law, systems of weights and measures, social welfare arrangements and brought order to a lawless region. Unlike today's free traders, they were not averse to paying taxes, and were prepared to accept conditions of host countries such as fixed prices (as occurred for example with the Cologne Hansa in London in 1157). As a result of their activities, the north of Europe became a centre of wealth creation, peace and civilised progress. How different, for example, to modern Latin America, which has been subjected to forty years of free market experimentation under the guidance of US theoreticians whose value to the region can be measured by the fact that they have only been able to achieve local compliance by the use of violence, intimidation and wholesale murder.

The Hanseatic League may have been at times ruthless, but it arose in troubled times and faced equally ruthless enemies. It was prepared to risk much in defence of community values. As we face up to our own troubled times, as our modern robber barons extort economic concessions from the people through governments unwilling or unable to govern for the general good, we could do worse than to see the league as a guide; to learn from their mistakes, and their successes.

What lessons can we learn apart from those already outlined? We know the concept is alive and well in northern Europe; the US failed in its bid for a Baltic free trade zone despite the fact that the original Hanseatic cities reorganised in the 1980s to assist former Eastern bloc members and to carry out environmental initiatives. The US failure can be safely put down to historical awareness in the region (Hamburg, for example, still refers to itself as The Free and Hanseatic City of Hamburg) and a clear understanding there of the anti-community basis of modern free trade frameworks.

The thing to bear in mind is that the guilds used collective bargaining to establish a system within the economy, then went on to become the engine room of the economy, so perhaps the major lesson in all this is that it just might be that economic initiatives organised at the local or city level are the most effective and the most representative of community needs and aspirations.

It's worth examination. A parallel economy. It has a nice ring to it.

Dark Lords: An examination of the psychology behind free market theory

It's been said that the modern passion for free markets is a peculiarly Anglo-Saxon phenomenon because although global financial institutions and sundry think tanks give vocal support, the only governments to initially embrace market rule without reservation were those of Britain and its former colonies of North America New Zealand and Australia. But why would this be so? What is it in the culture of Britain that would give rise to an economic outlook so focused on short-term gain that it might well destroy itself and the social system that gave it birth?

The ruthless nature of free market philosophy, its utter disregard for the needs of the less capable must have its roots in some aspect of British history, some major factor not experienced by comparable nations. It's been assumed by many (including this writer) that this ruthlessness developed as a natural aspect of capitalism, but it was actually present much earlier. A typical example is the closure of the commons in England beginning in the 12th Century, (note that date!) the theft of the common lands on which communities depended for food, with subsequent deprivation forcing many to the towns and cities, creating a ready and compliant work force for the emergence of industrialisation. This was a major factor in Britain jumping ahead of the field in converting to an industrial economy, aided by the reluctance of competitors to force agricultural workers into the cities as a source of cheap labour. The needs of the few were given higher value than those of the many, and economic theory was designed to serve only the few from a point very early in British history, but what was that point?

Prior to the Norman invasion, Anglo-Saxon society was distinguished for its cohesiveness built on an advanced system of local government, but the Normans reversed that with the introduction of military feudalism; centralised control of the land by a network of hastily built fortifications that dotted the countryside. The rigid stratification of society that followed the conquest was not necessarily William's original intention, even though the invasion

> was not, like the Saxon or Danish invasions, a national migration. It was an aristocratic conquest led by a man who won a kingdom for himself, distributed land among his followers…to gain a power unprecedented among European kings. [Emphasis added][1]

Of importance also,

> The resultant almost total replacement of an English with a Norman aristocracy was paralleled by a similar change of personnel among the upper clergy and administrative officers.[2]

His wish was to be recognised as the rightful heir of the last king of the West Saxon line, and to rule an Anglo-Norman state in which English and Norman could work together. But repeated rebellions prevented such an outcome, induced William to lay waste to vast areas of land that supported the rebels (a retribution so fierce the death toll and starvation aroused indignation and horror across Europe), and assisted in the creation of a ruling class and bureaucracy that saw the use of force against the populace as an acceptable tool for achieving an entirely new imperative; the utilisation of the nation's resources for the exclusive enjoyment of the few.

And use force they did. Not a hundred years had passed since the conquest when the Welsh were attacked in 1157, and by 1210 the Scots and Irish had suffered similar fates. But it was not only near neighbours that suffered from this drive. The English working class was also tested, finally rising in revolt in 1381, a revolt so effective the rulers were forced to negotiate, but which was put down by deceit and bloodshed. As well as a poll tax, 'probably the main grievance of the agricultural labourers and urban working classes was the Statute of Labourers (1351), which attempted to fix maximum wages during the labour shortage following the Black Death',[3] an early sign that the laws of economics would always be the preserve of the few.[4]

Though the revolt was put down, it showed that care had to be taken with domestic resources, so a pattern was begun of honing the fine arts of control and exploitation on near neighbours, to enable the real work of global imperialism to begin.[5]

Now it is true that the British were not alone in this, other European powers were equally determined when it came to domination and exploitation, but something about the British gave them an edge and left them not content with being mere colonisers. They set about establishing a global hegemony, a network of little Britains infused with British culture. Crucially, when the colonial era ended and the Brits departed, their structures and economic outlook in general remained, in contrast to the former colonies of Spain that have tried unsuccessfully for about a century to construct alternative economic and social frameworks, only to be thwarted by the military power of the USA. This clinging to all things British is a fine example of cultural hegemony as described by Gramsci, but is there an aspect to hegemony that Gramsci overlooked; did the British legacy contain a parasite?

Let's summarise the outlook of the Norman invaders. After the conquest they found themselves in control of a land in constant rebellion for a considerable period, a military state was formed, a siege mentality grew, the use of brutal force against the people became the norm, and a strong sense of 'otherness' developed, a sense that the masses were a lesser species, a resource to be utilised for the benefit of the conquerors. This was compounded by the loss of Normandy about one hundred and fifty years after the invasion, a shattering loss that increased the sense of isolation of the Normans whose ties to the Continent were severed. Now alone, now without roots or a sense of belonging, survival became paramount.

It seems to have gone unnoticed by historians that this mind-set survived the gradual absorption of the Normans into British society. This fear and suspicion, this seeing every man as an enemy, this ruthlessness and urge to power, sense of isolation and otherness, failure to see society as an organic whole, emerged intact as a pseudo-philosophy around four hundred years later, the philosophy of liberalism (economic individualism) as expounded by Hobbes and Locke. Hobbes' false view of society as a battleground with every man pitted against every other man still permeates liberal thinking today, and so strong was the urge to power in Locke's thinking that he openly advocated revolution to advance bourgeois interests. So liberalism with its fetish for free markets is not quite an Anglo-Saxon phenomenon as some have suggested, but is instead Anglo-Norman. Economic individualism, this deeply flawed outlook that with the benefit of hindsight we should half expect of an alienated people clinging to a delusion of superiority, has survived by its natural appeal to those of similarly retarded social instincts.

Of course the scenario presented here is beginning to look very much like 'meme theory' as described by Richard Dawkins (Professor for Public Understanding of Science at Oxford University), a meme being an idea, concept, or cultural feature which self-replicates, spreading from host to host and therefore subject to natural selection, a parasitical entity that has no 'purpose' other than survival. As Dawkins pointed out, the memes that survive best are those that actively encourage their own reproduction and spread as do certain religious beliefs, and clearly those pushing the cult of free markets and economic individualism have a similar zeal, a fundamentalist approach to spreading and enforcing the gospel of the market.[6]

So is the argument valid? Is the modern passion for free markets merely the visible symptom of a parasitical entity born of social crises unique to Britain, exported across the globe wherever the British put down roots, forced by natural selection to alter form, to adapt to changing environments, occasionally flourishing, never quite dying out, re-emerging in the late twentieth century to wreak havoc once again as the long-suffering people of Iraq can attest? (Remember that despite the democratic ideal being the final desperate justification for the conquest of Iraq, once the country was controlled by the Western forces privatisation occurred before democratisation.) It seems almost outlandish to attribute the present direction of the global economy to a military campaign that occurred in 1066, but the parallels between the outlook of the Normans and that of the marketeers, the determination of both to enforce an elitist economic agenda through a centralised government eager to exercise superior military might, are just too great to ignore. Furthermore, as we are looking at what was once a uniquely British phenomenon that must have its roots in British history only, no other incident or episode covers all the questions nearly as well. And while a link between the Normans and free markets at first seems tenuous at best, keep in mind that the free market aspect is merely the latest window dressing for a consistent underlying economic agenda that is socially unacceptable and therefore in constant need of repackaging to neutralise community resistance.

Meme theory might not adequately explain the crude market Darwinism of an individual such as Herbert Spencer, but it would explain why such an outrageous outlook still enjoys significant unspoken support and has become the basis of the Australian Liberal government's industrial relations reforms. It would explain why Charles Darwin's declaration that mankind's social instincts are primary and individual instincts secondary[7] was and still is ignored by the British establishment. It would explain, bearing in mind that a meme's primary 'concern' is survival, the motives of the British diplomat who told his US counterpart, once Britain had slipped from its position of pre-eminence, that the Brits were passing the baton to the US. It explains Winston Churchill's belief in 'the Anglo-sphere', a world dominated by British and US culture. (The Anglo-sphere is a concept still active in the minds of such luminaries as Conrad Black.) It explains why market rule and military power are so tightly interwoven as to be two sides of the one coin, why the liberal deity Competition is, as William Morris pointed out, merely a veiled form of warfare, why liberals cannot live peacefully alongside rival political models and why they had to invent an enemy when the Cold War ended. It explains their obsession with eroding social infrastructure and evaluating everything in economic terms, why liberalism evolved an extreme offshoot, libertarianism, and why libertarians such as Hayek became enamoured of British culture and history. It would even explain why ordinary Britons, those unmoved by elitist aspirations, still feel aggrieved; still feel a sense of loss resulting from the events of 1066. Maybe a counter-meme exists, a meme of resistance to 'normanisation' with its intolerance, its divisiveness, its unquenchable thirst for conflict with enemies both without and within. Perhaps Tolkien, consciously or unconsciously, struck a chord with the public by expressing this meme of resistance in his *Lord of the Rings*, a tale of the determination of little folk to not be trampled underfoot, to preserve simple wholesome values in harmony with the natural world, to reject the lure of power and maintain a sense of community.

Meme theory would certainly explain why the present fortress of liberalism, the corporation, has many of the features of the Anglo-Norman state, for the corporation is expansionist, fearful of competitors, devoid of social empathy or obligation, exercising absolute centralised control over a workforce that is technically free but in practice in a position of vassalage, and why, like the Anglo-Norman state, the corporation is concerned with two priorities only; distributing wealth to an elite group, and survival.

Henrietta Leyser, historian at Oxford University, made the point on the television documentary *The Normans, a Dynasty that Changed the World*[8] that the suspicion still felt by the East towards the West can be put squarely at the feet of the Normans for the role they played in the Crusades. Sadly that's only the half of it. The repeated attacks on the World Trade Centre show that the economic legacy of the Normans is the catalyst today not just for ill-feeling, but for what is seen as a battle for survival.

Notes

As I understand meme theory, a meme does not itself adapt to changing conditions as it has no consciousness, instead the reverse is the case, as a self-replicating entity circumstances change it over time. That seems a little hard to grasp, but presumably as each person expresses a meme in a slightly different way, those expressions that more readily find a receptive host will have the greater chance of survival and spread. This means that we should see incremental change over time, and so we do with for example, some varieties of popular Christianity. That's also the case with free market ideology. Its proponents in the late nineteenth century were capable of expressing the most callous disregard for the freely admitted suffering of those unable to compete economically, were capable of almost celebrating their misfortune. However as the world has become more civilised in outlook, more civilised justifications, albeit still fraudulent, had to be found. Dawkins's analogy of a meme as a virus or parasite is particularly apt in this case. Just as some of us have a resistance to certain infections, so some of us are resistant to the enticements of free market rhetoric. And just as a virus or parasite has the potential to cripple or kill its host, so free market ideology with its fixation on individual wants rather than needs, has the potential to cripple human society as we know it. (My embrace of meme theory should not be taken as a similar endorsement of Dawkins's fallacious theory of selfish genes.)

It would be a mistake to assume, as marketeers would have us believe, that the present dominance of free market ideology is the culmination of an evolutionary process driven by an alleged need to consume, an inevitability against which resistance is futile. Capitalism based on the British model is in some cases adopted by those awed by its productivity and blind to its social consequences, is in some cases installed and maintained by force, but is in all cases flawed by an inherent process of alienation described so well by the great nineteenth century socialist thinkers. Now it might be intriguing, even useful to speculate as we have here as to the origin of that alienation, but the point to keep in mind is that other viable models of economic development exist.

References
1. Doris Mary Stenton, *English Society in the Early Middle Ages*, 4th edition, (Penguin 1965) pp. 13–14.
2. Norman Conquest, Encyclopaedia Britannica 2002, Standard Edition CD ROM.
3. Peasants' Revolt, Encyclopaedia Britannica 2002, Standard Edition CD ROM.
4. Barry Hughes, *Exit Full Employment* (Sydney, Angus and Robertson, 1980) p. 221. The sentence is worth quoting in full: 'Only when the pursuit of self-interest remains the preserve of the few does the system remain workable.'
5. Noam Chomsky, *Year 501, The Conquest Continues*, (London, Verso 1993) pp. 3, 7.
6. The term 'gospel of the market' has been taken up by most critics of free market ideology, but was possibly first used by its proponents, notably Bill

Clinton at the Asia-Pacific summit in Seattle where according to Chomsky he expounded his 'grand vision for Asia' bringing leaders together 'to preach the gospel of open markets and to secure America's foothold in the world's fastest growing economic community'. Noam Chomsky, Some Truths and Myths About Free Market Rhetoric, Lies of Our Times, 7 January 1994.

7. In his *Descent of Man*, available online at Project Gutenberg, Charles Darwin devoted two full chapters, 4 and 5, to the importance of sociality in evolution and concluded that in humans, as in most other animals, the social instinct is primary and the individual instinct secondary.

8. *Lost Worlds – The Normans, a Dynasty That Changed the World*, a three-part British documentary presented by Melvyn Bragg, was broadcast on SBS Australia in April 2005.

Postscript

Shortly after 'Dark Lords' was published in *State of Nature* (an earlier version was published in *Voice* March 2006), I came across the 24th annual John Bonython Lecture delivered by Lawrence M. Mead of the Department of Politics at New York University to The Centre For Independent Studies, an Australian right-wing think tank, on 27 June 2007. His lecture was titled 'Anglo Primacy at the End of History: The Deep Roots of Power'. Mead's basic theme was that US supremacy was embedded deep in British history and would continue indefinitely due to 'Anglo' exceptionalism. Though he ignored the immorality and hypocrisy involved in the Anglo pursuit of power, somehow seeing immorality as ethical conduct, the lecture confirmed the essence of the argument put in 'Dark Lords' that capitalism based on the British model is a parasitical aberration that has its roots in the Norman conquest of England. Mead argued the following:

- that British exceptionalism began in the twelfth century (that is, as soon as Britain was Normanised;
- that this cultural change is a virtue, and one that has been transplanted to the US, New Zealand and Australia (in other words it is a cultural entity or meme that spreads from host to host);
- that this cultural change is seen as having conferred superiority to the British in the field of economic organisation (therefore the

market economics that reigns supreme today, and is controlled, as Mead points out, by the Anglos, came directly from the Normans, so liberalism is in fact Normanism); and

- that this superiority gives Anglos the right to arrange the world to suit themselves, and to use force where necessary to achieve this (showing that the readiness of the Normans to use military force to achieve economic ends has not diminished with the passage of time).

Here are some short extracts:

And within Europe, Britain was again out in front. England achieves the rule of law in the twelfth century and government by consent in the thirteenth century—way ahead of any other large European state. This early development, I think, is the most fortunate thing that has ever happened in politics, since the Roman Empire. It is the essential reason why the Anglo countries are so prosperous and secure today. Britain's precocious regime was then a principal reason why the country developed its effective market economy, and then grew rich, and then projected that power to the ends of the earth. [Mead's emphasis]

And among Western countries, it's not just America but all the Anglo nations that stand supreme. By Anglo nations I mean Britain and all the countries that were settled chiefly from Britain—The U.S. but also Australia, Canada, and New Zealand. Not only are these, as a group, the richest of all countries—they are also more or less running the world.

You need a strong and honest government to run an effective market economy. And you need it to translate wealth into military power and to project it abroad.

All of our potential rivals are weak in one or another of the dimensions I have discussed. Either they lack a native propensity for capitalism, or they lack an individualist society, or they lack good government. Only America and the other Anglo countries have all these assets. So today, they are still running the world, and I see no end to that any time soon.

For full text go to http://www.cis.org.au/Media/releases/Bonython_07.pdf

Puppies and Other Important People

When Avigail Abarbenel suggested in *Voice* 7 that 'right wing thinking is not a reasonable political alternative but an expression of a sickness', I expected that such a bold statement would provoke a fascinating flurry of responses for and against. I waited in vain, but the subject is so important that it deserves further discussion.

I have a couple of pups who play together, their favourite game beginning when one picks up a highly desirable and useful object such as an old corn cob, a piece of rope or a stick. It then parades in front of the other with a jaunty air until a chase ensues, with the chaser attempting to dispossess the other. If this fails, the loser will look for something equally desirable, and parade with it in an attempt to reverse the roles. We've all seen wildlife documentaries in which lion cubs or young chimps play similar games, with parents looking on with amused indifference. It seems safe to assume, therefore, that competitive acquisitiveness is a function of the immature offspring of the higher mammals, and possibly some lower orders of species. It's a phase they grow out of, a stepping stone on the pathway to maturity and wisdom. But not according to our respected economic scientists and cultural managers, who tell us that this activity is actually the driver behind civilisation as we know it. The fact that it has driven other species nowhere at all seems to have escaped their notice.

Assertions regarding the wholesomeness of competitive acquisitiveness have been around for quite a while As in this from von Hayek, the father of modern free market activism

> the universal mover in human nature, selflove, may receive such a direction…as to promote the public interest by those efforts it shall make towards pursuing its own.

Such assertions have been used to denigrate less technology-oriented peoples, and this wholesomeness has been most useful in justifying their subjugation with a view to their further education. The accompanying exploitation and expropriation has no doubt been intended only as a practical demonstration of the benefits of acquiring a civilised outlook. The concept has not matured or evolved over the years, it's merely rehashed to suit the occasion.

But this bourgeois outlook does have a certain childish logic to it, and a childish morality. There's something about achieving dominance that converts principles and ethics into irrelevancies. We've seen it in kings, popes, dictators and now the bourgeoisie. At some point on the path to dominance, the dominant group abandons its clearly understood obligations and intentions with respect to the rest of society (the cooperation of the masses being essential to their aims) and assumes that its own interests are society's interests. Just as children and puppies believe that the universe revolves around them and that, by simply wishing something away, reality can be changed. The present dominance of the bourgeoisie means that it is automatically assumed, without the need for analysis or reflection, that what's good for the business class is good for society. And just as kings assumed that their interests were the people's interests and constructed the divine right of kings as an elaborate justification for their betrayal of the people's trust, so the bourgeoisie have constructed a similarly ridiculous and childish justification for their betrayal of the democratic ideals they claim to espouse – an irrational reverence for the unfettered operation of market forces. Furthermore, just as kings knew their claims to be erroneous and had no respect for divine standards, so the bourgeoisie pay lip service only to market forces, regulating them ruthlessly when the need for profit demands. (I could barely contain my delight when I saw Chris Corrigan complaining bitterly to an interviewer and calling for re-regulation because the privatisation of airports was affecting his business.) This is policy making at the level of the schoolyard; policy-making aimed at instant gratification coupled with the childish hope that their present run of good fortune will last forever.

In short, Avigail was right. We are governed by those of stunted intellectual development, by strutting pups with corncobs in their mouths. But this raises the question as to how these clowns have been able to maintain their circus act for so long. The answer is: with the assistance of an intellectual class that has one outstanding weakness – an overwhelming inner need to be subservient. To fawn, to flatter, to constantly seek nods of approval from their masters. Small pups rolling over for larger ones. They devote a lifetime of service to the powerful, by disseminating a constant stream of disinformation. Here's an example.

In a column in *The Weekend Australian* of 18 December 2004, a certain Cameron Stewart, standing in as understudy for that martinet (or should that be marionette, I just can't decide) of the market Paul 'The Pontiff' Kelly, bemoaned the increasing risk of nuclear weapons proliferation that comes with the spread of new technologies. Said Stewart,

> Many smaller countries have the know-how, material and therefore the potential to use their legitimate nuclear facilities to make weapons grade fuel if they wish.

Now it just happens that anti-nuclear lobby groups have argued for decades, until blue in the face, that the promotion of nuclear power generation would lead to weapons proliferation. For their trouble they were ridiculed, but now are proved right. However, Stewart has learned well from the Pontiff. There was not a hint of acknowledgement that anti-nuclear groups even existed, let alone predicted this outcome. That's the beauty of right-wing blindness. When things go wrong, when you get caught out, it's never your fault. In this case, according to Stewart, the fault lies with 'technological advances, a changing security environment, and the failure of countries to comply with international law'. Funny that. That's just about chapter and verse for the very risk factors cited by anti-nuclear groups. No connection at all seen by Stewart to greed and shortsightedness. Yet I can still see the then deputy PM Doug Anthony pleading for the opening of new uranium mines on the irrefutably logical grounds that if we did not make a profit from uranium sales then someone else would. And all the time declaring nuclear power to be safe and clean. 'Let's make a killing while we can' might not have been his exact words, but that was his drift, and that attitude, if Stewart's alarm call can be believed, is looking less metaphorical by the day.

Unless of course, this whole exercise by Stewart was only intended to get us onside for an impending invasion of Iran. Would a Murdoch publication do that? Whether it was a case of demonizing the next 'official enemy' or covering up for a major blunder, the article was a great example of the lengths to which the liberal-democratic propaganda machine will go, in order to constantly mould public opinion and cloud reality.

But back to our pups. The thing to bear in mind about competitive acquisitiveness is that its adherents simply cannot give it up. There's too much at stake. If they were to concede that consumerism is not sustainable, it would mean the death of capitalism in any recognisable form. Their system is dependent on perpetual growth so that the illusion of economic health can be maintained. Just watch how current conventional wisdom regarding the need for balanced budgets will be jettisoned if the global economy goes into serious decline. Keynesian 'pump priming' that has been relegated to the realms of voodoo economics will be magically rediscovered, and governments not willing to use debt to promote growth will be castigated by those who affect to despise Keynes today. And the Pontiff will be first on board, the first to man the pump. Well, to bark the orders at least. While ever there's a corn cob to strut with, all available means will be used to preserve the illusion that market rule is the only option.

Liberty, Equality, Fraternity

At a conference on social policy hosted by the UNSW in 1999, the keynote speaker Professor Jill Roe gave a particularly interesting presentation in which she suggested that despite the present dominance of free market thinking, 'Liberty, Equality and Fraternity have passed into the parlance of modernity, and...are now well-nigh indestructible.' Her main concern was to explain that at this period in time liberty, in its narrow form of economic liberty, is taking centre stage to the temporary detriment of the other two values, and while this was a valuable observation, the section quoted above has greater significance and leads to other important areas of discussion.

The fact that liberty equality and fraternity have been embraced by people of different cultures and different stages of economic development seems to indicate that universal values exist that link people across the globe. Other examples are not hard to find. Apparently, surveys have shown that most Americans believe 'from each according to his ability, to each according to his need' to be a part of the US Constitution, so logical is the proposition and so universal in appeal. Then there's the recent case of the co-presenter of a popular TV breakfast show in this country who began his broadcasting career as a commentator on financial affairs and could reasonably be expected to follow current market orientation yet campaigned strongly on the program for the budget surplus to be spent on health and education rather than tax cuts, demonstrating Jill Roe's point that the values of eighteenth century revolutionaries have indeed become mainstream and cross all boundaries.

It is true that the revolutionary slogan 'Liberté, Egalité, Fraternité' was heavily loaded with bourgeois connotations, and true that the middle-class revolutionaries who took control in France had little sympathy for the democratic aspirations of the French people at large.

But the reality is that slogans foster simple sentiments, and at face value these are radical anti-establishment concepts. As a result, they have become a message of hope for oppressed peoples everywhere, and in a strange twist of fate they have become a message of hope for those who now struggle under bourgeois hegemony.

But surely for socialists liberty implies liberating others, equality implies raising others up, and fraternity implies bonds of sympathy or solidarity. These are spiritual values, they are not self-centred concepts. They are largely outgoing, unselfish and thoughtful of the needs of others. These are the values that have now come to define the socialist outlook, not necessarily because they have been articulated as such, but because these are the concepts considered most dangerous by the dominant class. Yet how can our regard for strangers we will never meet, a regard so deep it can lead to extremes of feeling such as grief, anger and joy, have anything but a spiritual basis?

The problem with using the word 'spiritual' is that it has, for so many people, too close an association with the fables and hypocrisies of the Christian tradition. This is a view so widely held on the left that it has been an impediment to the evolution of socialist thought and to a wider acceptance of socialism itself. Worse still, an unnecessary, irrelevant and very public preoccupation with atheism/agnosticism has enabled its enemies to successfully depict socialism as being soulless and cruel. Advocates of socialism have stood impotent in the face of this campaign, bound by entanglements of their own creation, helpless as they watch the mendacious and the murderous take the high moral ground. If that was not tragic and ironic enough, those who have denied and decried Christianity the loudest have accepted without question its outrageous claims to exclusivity. As if there is no spirituality apart from the Christian faith, no philosophical base from which to fight back.

But consider the following from the Eastern tradition:

'Behold but One in all things.' – Kabir, AD 1500

'Be unselfish and kind, and give aid to all… As you make the

universe, so it becomes [Marx would have loved that] Break away from all relationships of country, status, caste and its duties [and that]'
– Hindu text, the Devikalottara

'All creatures and I together are one.' – Chuang Tzu, AD 300

All socialism, all pure socialism.

Now I'm not suggesting for a moment that the sacred texts of the East are but thinly disguised doctrines of socialism. Rather, that the defining values of socialism – liberty, equality, fraternity – have a link to Eastern philosophy that is direct and concrete.

If I can be so bold (or reckless) as to summarise Eastern philosophy in a single sentence, it could arguably go as follows: equality and fraternity are eternal values that are actualised during a process of liberation which is the overriding objective. This statement will raise a few eyebrows and possibly a few hackles as equality and fraternity are not terms in common use in Eastern thought.[1] But surely the frequent injunctions against inflicting harm, or the bodhisattva vow to liberate all sentient beings, or the dharmadhatu doctrine of the interdependence of all things, just to name a few, are all variations of these themes, developments and refinements that take equality and fraternity to another level. So in other words, the aspirations of the time-honoured search for truth that we see in the Eastern tradition are almost identical to the socialist impulse, merely being pursued at a different level of human experience.

Still not convinced? Check this out.

[As a]n integral part of collective existence, man feels his dignity at the same time in himself and in others, and thus carries in his heart the principle of a morality superior to himself. This principle does not come from outside; it is secreted within him, it is immanent. It constitutes his essence… It is the true form of the human spirit, a form which takes shape and grows towards perfection…

This could be a Buddhist philosopher discoursing on the subject of the Self, but is actually Pierre-Joseph Proudhon pondering the sense of justice that he believed lies at the core of our being. Proudhon was the father of libertarian socialism or anarchism, the libertarians at that time being locked in a struggle for supremacy with the authoritarian strain advocated by Marx. The Marxists eventually took control of the global push to socialism, and even that outcome is consistent with our theme. As liberation is the prime objective of Eastern philosophy and liberty, the foremost value in socialist thought,[2] we see here a theoretical explanation for our instinctive assumptions regarding the collapse of the Soviet system: a devotion to liberty that was less than impressive, falling far short of that required for a system which, if it is to be sustainable, must reflect the innermost yearnings of humankind.

On a more practical note, it's essential that socialism be presented as having a spiritual basis, if only to differentiate it from its capitalist competitor. This might seem nonsensical as the distinctions appear obvious, but look at it this way. All we have at present is a competition between rival ideologies of materialism, material productivity being the Stated aim of both systems. The free marketeers can't believe their luck that the battle lines are drawn this way as they know they're on a winner. Even Marx was under no illusions regarding the superiority of capitalist modes of production. The task for socialists is to promote the understanding that the civilising values of liberty, equality and fraternity have greater potential benefits than the accumulation of wealth, and to promote the undeniable fact that they can only be truly realised under a socialist system, as they are in conflict with the aims and more importantly the mechanisms of market economics, despite all the rhetoric to the contrary.

But let's shift back to our East/West connection and give the last word to Peter Arshinov, who fought with Nestor Mahkno's heroic revolutionary army of the Ukraine against the Tsar, the Germans and the Bolsheviks, and who, like Proudhon, expresses the universality and profundity of true socialist thought:

> Look into the depths of your own being, seek out the truth and realise it yourselves, you will find it nowhere else.

Notes

1. The Dalai Lama seems to be an exception to the rule, being prepared to comment on political affairs in general, referring to himself as 'half-Buddhist, half-Marxist', and stating that 'All sentient beings should be looked on as equal.'

2. English socialism was profoundly influenced by the libertarianism of Godwin, as in the works of William Morris, Oscar Wilde, Bernard Shaw and H.G. Wells, while Proudhon was even more influential on the Continent, inspiring the First International and the Spanish socialists among others. There was even a libertarian strain in the US, invigorated by European immigrants, but eventually suppressed by state-sanctioned violence and 'judicial activism'.

The Collective Illusion

Bertrand Russell once described Western philosophy as a 'No-Man's Land between theology and science', which may have been a little harsh, but it has certainly been notable for speculation and difference of opinion.

Eastern philosophy, on the other hand, has been more cohesive, with the growth of different schools certainly, but all resting on common principles and all devoted to a common goal. One of these principles holds that the universe is comprised of layers of reality, and although this might seem a trifle odd, it should be remembered that Westerners claiming adherence to any faith at all believe in at least two such layers.

While readers might be excused for thinking that these issues are rather esoteric and hardly worth the bother, there is a concept of Eastern philosophy that would be of great value to the West if better known and understood. I refer to the concept of the collective illusion (maya in Eastern philosophy) and believe awareness of it to be of some significance as the failure of this awareness to take root in the Western consciousness has had a major influence on human social development. So just what is maya?

In the spiritual sense, maya is that influence which attaches us to a common illusion, which prevents us knowing our essential nature by reinforcing the belief that (a) the physical universe is the only reality, and (b) we are separate and distinct entities within that reality. For a thought system concerned with various layers of reality, this is a concept of great significance, because the conquest of maya then becomes the whole purpose of philosophical endeavour, the bridge to ultimate truth. Now this approach to philosophical inquiry is in general terms almost unknown in the West, but it was known to some of the ancient Greeks and did feature strongly in Plato's *Republic*. In his parable of the cave in Book VII, Plato described the journey of the individual from ignorance to awareness in terms consistent with the Eastern understanding of maya, but unfortunately this feature of his best known work has been virtually disregarded. Russell, for example, in his *History of Western Philosophy* gave a brief description of the parable, referred to it merely as a simile, attempted almost no discussion and moved on to more important matters. His reluctance to pursue and develop this line of thinking is no doubt explained by his atheism, a subject to which we will return later.

Perhaps the closest we have come to a modern Western (and almost by definition materialistic) explanation of the collective illusion was that provided by the Italian Marxist Antonio Gramsci with his interpretation of hegemony. Hegemony, according to Gramsci, is the situation that exists when a dominated people accept the values and priorities of the ruling class as being valid and legitimate, possibly worth fighting and dying for, even though the resulting policies might be discriminatory and exploitative to their cost. In such a situation there exists for the exploited class an illusion of justice and natural order which is constantly reinforced to prevent the possibility of a desire for change. Hence the link to the collective illusion of maya in which we are discouraged from considering the possibility that there might be more to life than mere physical existence as determined by our sensory perception. Just as knowledge of Plato's parable has been restricted to prevent spiritual development independent of organised religion, so an understanding of hegemony is not widespread or encouraged, due to the fact that mere awareness of the concept undermines the power of influential institutions. It is of no small significance that dictionary definitions refer only to the narrow Greek derivation pertaining to leadership ('hegemon': leader) with not a hint of underlying injustice or misplaced loyalty. While modern expanded meanings are generally welcomed by compilers of dictionaries and can even be a source of some professional pride, it seems that when it comes to dispelling the illusions of class with the associated possibility of offending the powerful, there are definite limits to liberal scholarship.

While we're on that note, Gramsci made a further contribution to our understanding by pointing out the essential role of an intellectual class in organising the consent of the masses in support of the dominant class. This is the role played for example by media commentators, or organisers of school curricula who deliberately avoid highlighting, in courses purporting to be history, the contributions to social evolution made by popular movements of dissent.

His explanation of hegemony is particularly relevant today as we see the free market values and priorities of a wealthy business class being accepted by governments of all persuasions as being appropriate values for all members of society. And as those priorities include perpetuating the lie that we are best served by seeing ourselves as independent economic units, so we see the quite remarkable connection between free market economics and the illusions of maya in which individuals are also encouraged to see themselves as separate entities, in that case distinct from their organic connection to universal life.

With this in mind it may be worthwhile to consider the possibility that free market philosophy, being so intent on alienation of the individual and the subsequent destruction of the bonds of community, is actually the most effective manifestation of the collective illusion in human history, the ultimate expression of sterile materialism.

It's unfortunate that Gramsci and other Marxists who looked at the question of the collective illusion were unable to make a spiritual connection. Quite puzzling, in fact, given that their dialectical method is a tool designed for revealing contradictions and illusions, and that one of the basics of dialectical materialism holds that 'all natural phenomena are organically connected with, dependent on, and determined by, each other...no phenomenon in nature can be understood if taken by itself, isolated from surrounding phenomena...' one of a number of concepts held in common with Eastern philosophy.

Marx himself was possibly the greatest of this group with his exposure of the illusions of class on which modern economic doctrine is founded, a truly monumental effort, but his rival, the powerful Russian thinker Mikhail Bakunin is in some ways a more interesting example. In *God and The State* he made the stunning observation that the Satan of the Old Testament Garden of Eden story was the first free thinker in that he offered mankind both the key to knowledge and the spirit to rebel. While Bakunin obviously knew the Eden story was a myth, the point he missed was that this was an allegory concerning maya, the ignorance dispelled by Satan being the illusion that Eden (the material world) was the only reality. (The knowledge of good and evil referred to in Genesis is a metaphor to describe the increased awareness that results from the breaking down of illusions.) The whole tone of Bakunin's text suggests that he believed that fables were all religion could offer, and there are historical reasons for this. The Church has been quite happy, for reasons of its own, to feed fables to the faithful for most of its history, in the process allowing itself to be used, to become part of the collective hegemonic illusion associated first with the divine right of kings, later with the rise of the 'liberal-democratic' state, and consequently a legitimate target for the iconoclasts.

Bakunin admitted that his anger at the Church for its part in the class illusion was one of his prime motivations and the reason for his atheism. He could not find it in himself to see any redeeming features in an organisation so oppressive of mankind's natural urge for freedom, and so saw an attack on the central concept of the Church, the existence of God, as a means of exposing its illusions. We can hardly criticise him for that, and perhaps Bakunin's situation holds the key to that puzzling aspect of the dialectical method referred to previously. We are all products of our particular era, and necessarily display characteristics peculiar to our era. So too with dialectical materialism, which developed in the grim shadow of the twin monoliths of Church and State and inevitably reflected a desire for a withering away of both. Remember that in the time of Marx and Bakunin the Church was still backing the divine right of kings, with all the oppression and suffering which that entailed.

But apart from that, Bakunin's explanation of our early development is also intriguing. He stated that

Our first ancestors, near relatives of apes, omnivorous, intelligent and ferocious beasts, were endowed in a higher degree than other species with two precious faculties – the power to think and the desire to rebel.

The question that poses is this: in the primitive world of our early ancestors, a world ruled not by institutions but only by natural forces, what was there to rebel against but the illusions of existence? The answer of course is that we chose to rebel against the forces of nature (by use of fire, then agriculture, irrigation and so on), in the process overlooking the possibility that those forces, while undoubtedly real, may have an illusory aspect.

For example, we cling desperately to the apparent solidity of the material world, even though we have known for almost a century now that atoms are composed mostly of empty space (Rutherford, 1911) and that the solidity of objects is an illusion produced by electrical charges associated with particles that are themselves in essence no more than waves or bundles of energy. (de Broglie, 1924, confirmed 1927). Knowing this, we continue to go about our daily activities on the basis of what our imperfect senses tell us of the physical world. The things we touch, hear, smell, see and taste constitute our reality. We see, therefore we believe. Which is fine from the point of view of practicality. But in this case practicality does not equate with reality, and one of the outcomes of this practicality is that it distracts us from being aware of or even considering, our essential nature.

Science has not only shown us the existence of other realities beyond our sense perception, such as radio waves, it has enabled us to use those realities to revolutionise our lives. Are we so conceited as to believe that we now know all, that no further realities await discovery? The plain fact is that science has proved one of the great concepts of Eastern philosophy, that the universe is comprised of layers of reality. Peeling back the corresponding layers of illusion always was and still is the great challenge for humankind, but science can only do so much. The social illusions that we have created ourselves, the relations that we accept as constants despite being proved to be transitory by the giant thinkers of the nineteenth century, are in some ways harder to ditch.

And so it's rather sad that we in the West are not more familiar with the concept of the collective illusion. Armed with that awareness, we might have been able to resist the worst excesses of the advertising industry with its creation of artificial wants and resultant pollution of our physical and emotional lives. We might have been able to prevent the manufacturing of our consent to go to war against an impoverished Third World people portrayed as a threat to world peace. We might have resisted the siren call of free market selfishness using the principle that society is an organic whole and that an injury to one member of society is an injury to us all. We still can.

And while I doubt that the ancients had modern advertising and mass propaganda in mind when they explained the collective illusion, I'm sure they would not mind us using the concept in the struggle for a better world.

Rethinking the Counterculture

In August 2006 SBS screened a documentary titled *Commune*, which featured a Californian community established in the late 1960s. It provided a fascinating insight into the thinking behind a social experiment that is sure to play a more significant role in the future as the consequences of consumerism become apparent even to those who are presently in denial.

The founders of the commune were a penniless group who approached pop stars and Hollywood personalities who they believed were enriching themselves from the counterculture that was in full swing at the time. They requested that these show business types put something back into the movement by contributing hard cash so that a commune could be established on the basis of their slogan 'free land for free people'. As a result, Black Bear Ranch was bought and became home for hundreds of people over the years. It's still serving that purpose today, with the legal title to the land arranged to ensure perpetuity.

One of the interesting attitudes displayed by the founders was the general acceptance by both sexes that gender determined work roles and that therefore men and women working together was unacceptable. This prejudice was jettisoned after a period, but as these people represented the freest of free thinkers at the time, it shows how far we have come in forty years.

Another of the more remarkable attitudes in the early period was an apparent need for conformity within this group of non-conformists, to the extent that one member's desire to be involved in art work was criticised as being anti-social as it necessitated individual creativity and could be construed as being antithetical to community activity.

Another naïve attitude involved an assumption by individuals that all other members came to the commune for the same reason as themselves. There was apparently no discussion as to the philosophical motivations for communal living, no analysis or reflection or consensus sought as to how an alternative social arrangement could best be made viable. It seems that it was tacitly agreed that the consumer society was morally bankrupt and that to adopt an alternative, any alternative, was sufficient. Because there was no coherent philosophy behind the establishment of the community, the founders eventually drifted away to pursue activities in mainstream society. Yet all retained links to the group and the community still functions, which shows that some things, perhaps many things, were instinctively done correctly or had a worthwhile foundation.

One interesting snippet was the chance remark by one of the founders that he was the grandson of the philosopher and educator Herbert Marcuse, which led me to look into the work of Marcuse who at that time was influential in the thinking of the 'New Left'. Unlike some other Marxist writers whose works require constant reference to a quality dictionary, Marcuse is readable and relevant. Some of his insights are quite exceptional. For example, not only did he detect the liberalising potential in Soviet life that surfaced about twenty years later under Gorbachev, he also saw the totalitarian potential of liberal democracy as far back as the 1960s, and when questioned after a lecture correctly predicted the means by which this would be put into effect:

> The new fascism – if it comes – will be very different from the old fascism. History does not repeat itself so easily. When I speak of the rise of fascism I mean, with regard to America, for example, that the strength of those who support the cutback of existing civil and political liberties will grow to the point where the Congress can institute repressive legislation that is very effective. That is...it can mean that the masses support increasingly actively a tendency that confines whatever scope still exists in democracy, thus increasingly weakening the opposition.

Not a bad forecast of the conditions that gave rise to the PATRIOT Act, considering that the world was a completely different place in the 1960s.

When asked about the right to resist the dominant class, the answer Marcuse gave was also particularly resonant with the conditions prevailing in the twenty-first century:

> Tolerance toward that which is radically evil now appears as good because it serves the cohesion of the whole on the road to affluence or more affluence. The toleration of the systematic dulling of children and adults alike by publicity and propaganda, the release of destructiveness in aggressive driving, the recruitment for and training of special forces, the impotent and benevolent tolerance toward outright deception in merchandizing, waste, and planned obsolescence are not distortions and aberrations, they are the essence of a system which fosters tolerance as a means for perpetuating the struggle for existence and suppressing the alternatives. The authorities in education, morals, and psychology are vociferous against the increase in juvenile delinquency; they are less vociferous against the proud presentation, in word and deed and pictures, of ever more powerful missiles, rockets, bombs-- the mature delinquency of a whole civilization.

He then made a most important point:

> The doctrine of the right of resistance has always asserted that appealing to the right of resistance is an appeal to a higher law which has universal validity, that is, which goes beyond the self-defined right and privilege of a particular group... If we appeal to humanity's right to peace, to humanity's right to abolish exploitation and oppression, we are not talking about self-defined, special, group interests, but rather and in fact interests demonstrable as universal rights. That is why we can and should lay claim today to the right of resistance as more than a relative right.

He went on,

> Thus, within a repressive society, even progressive movements threaten to turn into their opposite to the degree to which they accept the rules of the game. To take a most controversial case: the exercise of political rights such as voting, letter-writing to the press, to Senators, etc., protest-demonstrations with a priori renunciation of counter-violence, in a society of total administration serves to strengthen

this administration by testifying to the existence of democratic liberties which, in reality, have changed their content and lost their effectiveness. In such a case, freedom of opinion, of assembly, of speech, becomes an instrument for absolving servitude.

We saw the truth of this when the Howard government simply ignored public protest over its plans to assist in the destruction of Iraq. The government tolerated the protests because they performed a useful function; that is, they allowed the people to let off steam, and in so doing perpetuated the illusion of a successful working democracy. Yet it's also true that just a few years earlier the Multilateral Agreement on Investment, which would have handed effective control of global governance to corporate investors and speculators, was derailed by public protest. The MAI, if enacted, would have guaranteed the safety of international investment by making governments – that is, taxpayers – responsible for a range of losses incurred, and would have prevented governments from carrying out social programs that impinged at all on profits.

So clearly the people have the power, if only potentially, to influence the course of events. The problem in an era of mass communication and relentless indoctrination is to harness that potential and the chances are that only in exceptional circumstances such as the MAI will that occur.

Meanwhile, just as Marcuse also predicted, attempts are under way behind closed doors for the programs outlined in the MAI to be achieved through existing institutions such as the WTO and the IMF with no public input. (See Dr Sharon Beder's excellent book *Suiting Themselves – How Corporations Drive the Global Agenda*. Dr Beder is an Australian who writes in the concise factual style of another Aussie great, the late Alex Carey.)

So what's the answer? If as Marcuse predicted it's not so much governments but the institutions behind them that have become the vehicle for undermining democratic aspirations, if our only political option is to elect a different government that will follow roughly the same agenda as its predecessor, if dissent is of marginal utility and may even serve to entrench the dominant class, where do we go from here? The answer might lie in the *Commune* documentary.

It might seem a paradox, but the value of such communities, the value of a commitment to voluntary association, to mutual goals, collective action and mutual aid, is that ultimately individuals are empowered and individuality enhanced. Better still, this empowerment of individuals goes hand in hand with the disempowerment of the institutions of domination, for one cannot occur without the other. Mainstream culture claims to represent the historic triumph of individual rights, but this is at odds with the reality of mass indoctrination, of social and economic alienation, of consumer choice being determined by corporate imperatives, of conforming to an ever narrowing world view. On the contrary, individuality is enhanced by participation, by interacting with others, by contributing to neighbourhood discussions and activities, by winning debates and by losing them and all the time looking on life as a process of continual enrichment through learning and giving. And we can learn from the clumsy groping for meaning that the people of Black Bear Ranch had to go through; we can now recognise that participating in the development of a counterculture is not merely a cool thing to do before settling down to a mainstream existence, it's the only sane and responsible long-term option. There will be no single answer to this problem. Different groups will find different methods, but that's what liberty is all about and the world will be richer for it. But a commitment to a culture of community will be no easy thing, and I think it's important as communities coalesce that they base their organisation on Marcuse's concept of universal values. Instead of a situation where members conform to a set of rules and regulations that might ultimately undermine the project, to encourage an ongoing enthusiasm for community activity they should instead commit to a set of agreed principles that have universal validity which can then be applied to the issues that will inevitably arise.

Would a trend towards voluntary association and mutual aid involve by necessity a move into a technological backwater? Not at all. The promoters of the consumer society would like us to think that modern technological advances are the products of capitalism, but the foundations of modern science and industrial innovation were laid long before capitalism emerged as a social force. Blast furnaces for steel production, advanced mathematics, marine navigation, building construction on a large scale, global trade and the like were all developed by community enterprise.

Would such a trend require communal living and, in the minds of some, a perceived loss of individuality? Not necessarily. Living cheek by jowl is not a pre-condition for a commitment to mutual aid. The most powerful force harnessed by capitalism is its power to isolate and alienate the individual, indeed this is how it operates, how it maintains a dominant role. Despite this, that crushing power is in one sense quite superficial, for all that's needed to neutralize it is a general rise in consciousness, of awareness. One of the features of this raised awareness is that it can appear spontaneously in response to certain conditions. A great example of this was given by Russell Ward in *The Australian Legend*, where he told of the social forces that developed on the early goldfields. Isolated from the State apparatus for ensuring law and order, the diggers organised their own. As Ward put it,

> The force of collective public opinion is demonstrated also by the fact that it, rather than state power, was responsible for maintaining order, of a sort, on the goldfields. Almost all contemporary observers agreed that this was so…

He then went on to give examples from the mining industry, including one that he witnessed himself as late as 1937. In short, he gave documented examples of voluntary association, mutual goals, mutual aid and collective action, all put in place and valued by people of the most individualistic outlook that it's possible to imagine.

One of the major problems of community life in the pre-industrial era was that it could be a stifling existence, a life ruled by the enforced need to conform to religious standards, to political and social tyranny, even to the whispering campaigns of neighbours. This was 'the idiocy of rural life' referred to by Marx. We were liberated from this to a degree by industrialization and city living, and by the idealistic drive of the Enlightenment with its regard for reason, freedom of conscience and tolerance. But with tolerance now being used, as Marcuse has shown, as a tool to subdue our urge for justice, a tool to perpetuate elitism and exploitation, we need a radical re-think. If we are to break the shackles of domination, and we must if we are to leave anything of value for the future, we have to redefine and re-position tolerance, giving it pride of place in a variety of styles of community living which, while being driven by the instinct for collective action and mutual aid, can only be successful if founded on individual choice, on the highest regard for diversity, on the libertarian ideal.

So what's different today from the conditions that gave rise to the counterculture movement of forty years ago, given that despite huge changes in the political landscape we are still facing the same problems – that is, frustration with both an immoral political ideology hell-bent on military aggression, and with a consumption-driven economy racing headlong towards extinction? The differences are subtle but important, giving cause for both cautious hope and alarm. The advent of internet communication means that those opting for community-based lifestyles are no longer isolated, so that the diversity essential for a healthy counterculture is now possible even to the extent of allowing geographical isolation while facilitating mutualism. The commune is now simply one option available, the range of options being limited only by our collective imagination. But unlike the 1960s, the addiction of consumerism is now not merely a theoretical problem that might impact some time in the future. Global warming and species depletion are realities that are accepted by all except those running the fossil fuel industry and the politicians they have bought, other influential promoters of consumerism who were previously in denial are slowly coming on board. But as individuals we have an obligation to embark on sustainable lifestyles right now, for to wait for political leaders to change course would be futile and ultimately fatal. The 1960s was just a trial run.

Conclusion

Universal values, following the lead of Herbert Marcuse, are those values that confer benefit or advantage to all peoples, no matter where they are located or situated. Universal values include such things as non-aggression, freedom from discrimination and so on. Their opposites are personal or sectional interests and priorities, those self-defined rights or privileges of a particular group, such as unlimited property acquisition, exploitation and appropriation, or religious intolerance.

Any political system that does not strive for universal values contains the seeds of its own demise, for such a system will always have its discontents, will always be eroded from within or be in conflict with those without. Liberal democracy is particularly at risk from this perspective, for it not only fails to embrace universal values, it actually regards such a concept as a threat to individual rights. To compound this unstable foundation, it actively pursues confrontation with rival political models.

So small has the world become and so dominant the priorities of liberalism, that liberal democracy is taking us all to the edge of destruction. It will take a global change in consciousness to bring us back from the edge, and we can only hope that the transition to the next phase in social evolution is relatively peaceful, as it well might be if there develops a general feeling that the time has come to move on. If it is not peaceful, our only consolation will be that the coming ascendancy of universal values will usher in a truly golden age. It will be up to the citizens of the day, however, to see that such a golden age endures, by ensuring that universal values are actively and unceasingly pursued. If there is one lesson to be learned from the struggle for liberty, it's that the struggle never ends.

Lightning Source UK Ltd.
Milton Keynes UK
UKOW04f1854011117
312033UK00001B/65/P